Presented to the Salvation Army
School for Officer Training
Central Territory, In Memory of

COMMISSIONER SAMUEL HEPBURN

THE DAILY STUDY BIBLE

THE ACTS
of the
APOSTLES

THE ACTS
of the
APOSTLES

Translated
with an Introduction and Interpretation
by

WILLIAM BARCLAY

THE WESTMINSTER PRESS
PHILADELPHIA

First published by The Saint Andrew Press
Edinburgh, Scotland
First Edition, January, 1953
Second Edition, December, 1955

Library of Congress Catalog Card No. 57-6030

Typeset in Great Britain
Printed in the United States of America

GENERAL INTRODUCTION

It may truly be said that this series of Daily Bible Studies began almost accidentally. A series which the Church of Scotland was using came to an end, and another series was immediately required. I was asked to write a volume on *Acts*, and, at the moment, had no intention beyond that. But one volume followed another, until the demand for one volume became a plan to write on the whole New Testament.

The translation which is given in each volume claims no special merit. It was included in order that the reader might be able to carry both the text of the New Testament and the comments on it wherever he went, and that he might be able to read it anywhere. While I was making the translation, the translations of Moffatt, Weymouth, and Knox were ever beside me. *The American Revised Standard Version, The Twentieth Century New Testament,* and *The New Testament in Plain English,* by Charles Kingsley Williams, have been in constant use. Since its publication, I have consistently consulted *The Authentic New Testament,* translated by Hugh J. Schonfield.

I cannot see another edition of these books going out to the public without expressing my very deep and sincere gratitude to the Church of Scotland Publications Committee for allowing me the privilege of first beginning, and then continuing, this series. And in particular I wish to express my very great gratitude to the convener, Rev. R. G. Macdonald, O.B.E., M.A., D.D., and to the committee's secretary and manager, Rev. Andrew McCosh, M.A., S.T.M., for constant encouragement and never-failing sympathy and help.

As these volumes went on, the idea of the whole series developed. The aim is to make the results of modern scholarship available to the non-technical reader in a form that it does not require a theological education to understand; and then to seek to make the teaching of the New Testament books relevant to life and work to-day. The whole aim of these books is summed up in Richard of Chichester's famous prayer; they are meant to enable men and women to know Jesus Christ more clearly, to love Him more dearly, and to follow Him more nearly. It is my prayer that they may do something to make that possible.

14430

THE ACTS OF THE APOSTLES

FOREWORD

It is partly in hope and partly in trepidation that I send out this little book. The circumstances of the case demanded that it should be written much more quickly than it should have been. The decision to end the " Life and Work " Daily Bible Readings and to begin this new undertaking was come to at a date which meant that the writing of this book has been a race against time in order that it should be ready for 1st January, 1953.

The translation was made, not because it claims any special merit, but rather in order that the reader might be able to carry both the text of Acts and the comments on it wherever he or she went. The commentary seeks to place in their background the events of Acts, and, by so doing, to make them live again ; and it aims, all the time, at making these events relevant for to-day.

The book has debts too many to mention. On every page it bears witness to its debt to the great five volume work, " The Beginnings of Christianity," that amazing commentary on Acts and store-house of information, edited by Foakes Jackson and Kirsopp Lake. Over and over again I have been indebted for flashes of insight and illumination to the recently published commentary on Acts by F. F. Bruce. Constantly beside me has been that unjustly forgotten commentary on Acts by T. M. Lindsay in the old Handbooks for Bible Classes Series ; it was in 1885 that it was first published, but there is still no better commentary for the non-technical student of Acts. I have further had the privilege of reading through the manuscript of an as yet unpublished commentary on Acts by my chief, Professor G. H. C. Macgregor.

It is my hope and prayer that this little book, with all its faults, may be used by God to awaken interest in His word and to lead those who use it to a better understanding of it.   WILLIAM BARCLAY.

Trinity College, Glasgow.

November 1952.

FOREWORD

THIS book has debts too many to mention. On every page it bears witness to its debt to the great five volume work, *The Beginnings of Christianity*, that amazing store-house of information, edited by Foakes Jackson and Kirsopp Lake. Over and over again I have been indebted for flashes of insight and illumination to F. F. Bruce's two commentaries on *Acts*, one on the Greek text, and one on the English text. Constantly beside me has been that unjustly forgotten commentary on *Acts* by T. M. Lindsay in the old Handbooks for Bible Classes Series; it was in 1885 that it was first published, but there is still no better commentary for the non-technical student of *Acts*. I have also found much help in the commentary on *Acts* in the Interpreter's Bible, by my chief, Professor G. H. C. Macgregor.

It is my hope and prayer that this little book, with all its faults, may be used by God to awaken interest in His word and to lead those who use it to a better understanding of that word.

TRINITY COLLEGE, GLASGOW.
November, 1955. WILLIAM BARCLAY.

THE ACTS OF THE APOSTLES

PRAYERS FOR USE BEFORE READING THE BIBLE

BLESSED Lord, by whose providence all holy scriptures were written and preserved for our instruction, give us grace to study them this and every day with patience and love. Strengthen our souls with the fulness of their divine teaching. Keep from us all pride and irreverence. Guide us in the deep things of Thy heavenly wisdom, and of Thy great mercy lead us by Thy Word unto everlasting life ; through Jesus Christ our Lord and Saviour. Amen.

Bishop Westcott.

ALMIGHTY and most merciful God, who hast given us the Bible to be the revelation of Thy great love to man, and of Thy power and will to save him : grant that our study of it may not be made vain by the callousness or carelessness of our hearts, but that by it we may be confirmed in penitence, lifted to hope, made strong for service, and above all, filled with the true knowledge of Thee and of Thy Son Jesus Christ. *George Adam Smith.*

BLESSED Lord, who hast caused all holy scriptures to be written for our learning : grant that we may in such wise hear, read, mark, learn and inwardly digest them, that by patience and comfort of Thy holy Word, we may embrace and ever hold fast the blessed hope of everlasting life, which Thou hast given us in our Saviour Jesus Christ.

The Book of Common Prayer.

PRAYERS FOR USE AFTER READING THE BIBLE

GRANT, O God, that that which I have read with my eyes and understood with my mind and received into my memory, I may now go out to show forth in my life. Grant that what I have learned by Thy grace I may use to Thy glory ; through Jesus Christ my Lord. Amen.

GRANT, O most merciful Father, that I may rise from the reading of Thy Book with a mind that is enlightened, with a will that is strengthened and with a heart that is stabbed broad awake to see the darkness of my sin and the wondrous glory of Thy love ; through Jesus Christ my Lord. Amen.

O THOU who art the Lord of all good life, grant that as I have read the story of those who lived heroically for Thee, I too may be kindled to serve Thee with grace and gallantry in my day and generation ; through Jesus Christ my Lord. Amen.

THE ACTS OF THE APOSTLES

CONTENTS

THE ACTS OF THE APOSTLES

CONTENTS

THE ACTS OF THE APOSTLES

CONTENTS

THE ACTS OF THE APOSTLES

CONTENTS

THE ACTS OF THE APOSTLES

INTRODUCTION

A Precious Book

In one sense it is true to say that the Book of Acts is the most important book in the New Testament. It is the simple truth that if we did not possess the Book of Acts, we would have, apart from what we could glean or deduce from the letters of Paul, no information whatever about the early Church. There are two ways of writing history. There is the way of the annalist, in which an attempt is made to trace the course of events from week to week and from day to day ; and there is the way in which a writer, as it were, opens a series of windows and gives us vivid glimpses of the great moments and personalities of any period. The second way is the way of the Book of Acts. We usually speak of *The Acts of the Apostles*. But the book neither gives nor claims to give an exhaustive account of the acts of the apostles. Apart from Paul only three apostles are mentioned in it. In Acts 12 : 2 we are told in one brief sentence that James, the brother of John, was executed by Herod. John appears in the narrative, but never speaks. It is only about Peter that the book gives us any real information, and very soon, as a leading character, he passes from the scene. But in the Greek there is no *The* before Acts ; the correct title is *Acts of Apostolic Men ;* and what Acts aims to do is to give us a series of typical exploits and adventures of the great heroic figures of the early Church.

The Writer of the Book

Although the book never says so, from the earliest times Luke has been held to be its writer. About Luke we really know very little ; there are only three references to him in the New Testament—Colossians 4 : 14, Philemon 24, 2 Timothy 4 : 11. From these three references we can say two things for sure. First, Luke was a doctor ; second, he was one of Paul's most valued helpers and most loyal friends, for he was a companion of Paul in his last imprisonment.

One thing we can deduce, the fact that Luke was a Gentile. Colossians 4 : 11 concludes a list of mentions and greetings from those who are of the circumcision ; that is, from Jews ; verse 12 begins a new list, and we naturally conclude that the new list are Gentiles. So then we have the very interesting fact that Luke is the only Gentile author in the New Testament.

We could have guessed that Luke was a doctor, because instinctively Lukes uses medical words. In Luke 4 : 35, when he tells of the man who had the spirit of an unclean devil, Luke uses the phrase " when the devil had thrown him," and the word he uses is the correct medical word for convulsions. In Luke 9 : 38 Luke draws the picture of the man who asked Jesus, " I beseech thee, look upon my son." The word used is the conventional word for a doctor paying a visit to a patient. The most interesting example of Luke's preference for a medical word is in the saying about the camel and the needle's eye. All the three gospel writers give us that saying. (Matthew 19 : 24 ; Mark 10 : 25 ; Luke 18 : 25). For the word needle both Mark and Matthew use the Greek word *raphis* which is the ordinary word for a tailor's or a household needle. Luke alone uses the word *belonè* which is the technical word for a surgeon's needle. Luke was a doctor, and a doctor's words came most naturally to his pen.

The Recipient of the Book

Luke wrote both his gospel and Acts to a man called Theophilus. (Luke 1 : 3, Acts 1 : 1). We can only guess who Theophilus was. In Luke 1 : 3 Luke calls him " most excellent Theophilus." The phrase really means " your excellency," and Theophilus must have been a man high up in the service of the Roman government. There are three possibilities concerning Theophilus.

(i) Just possibly Theophilus is not a real name at all. In those days it might well be dangerous to be a Christian. Theophilus comes from two Greek words, *theos* which means God, and *philein* which means to love. Just possibly Luke wrote this book to a lover of God, whose real name he did not use, because of the danger its use might cause.

(ii) As we have said it seems that Theophilus, if he was a real person, must have been a high government official. Perhaps Luke wrote the book to show him that Christianity was a lovely thing and that the Christians were good and fine people. Perhaps Acts is a defence of Christianity written to persuade a government official not to persecute the Christians.

(iii) There is a more romantic theory than either of these. Luke was a doctor and doctors in the ancient days were often slaves. Perhaps Luke was the doctor of Theophilus. Perhaps Theophilus had been ill even unto death, and perhaps by Luke's skill and devotion he was brought back to health. Perhaps in gratitude he gave Luke his freedom. Then, it may be, Luke wished to do something to show how grateful he was for this gift. The most precious thing he had was the story of Jesus, and maybe he wrote it and sent it to Theophilus because it was the most valuable thing he had to give him in return for the freedom he had received.

Luke's Aim in Writing Acts

When a man writes a book he does so for some reason, and maybe for more than one reason. Let us see now if we can find out some of the reasons why Luke wrote Acts.

(i) One of his reasons was to commend Christianity to the Roman government. Again and again he goes out of his way to show how courteous Roman magistrates were to Paul. In Acts 13 : 12 Sergius Paulus, the governor of Cyprus, becomes a Christian. In 18 : 12 Gallio is absolutely impartial in Corinth. In 16 : 35ff the magistrates at Philippi discover their mistake and apologise publicly to Paul. In 19 : 31 the Asiarchs in Ephesus are shown to be concerned that no harm should come to Paul. Luke was pointing out that in the years before he wrote the

Roman officials had often been well-disposed and always just and impartial to Christianity. Further, Luke takes pains to show that the Christians were good and loyal citizens, and that they had always been regarded as such. In Acts 18 : 14 Gallio declares that there is no question of wickedness or villainy. In 19 : 37 the secretary of Ephesus gives the Christians a good testimonial. In 23 : 29 Claudius Lysias is careful to say that he has nothing against Paul. In 25 : 25 Festus declares that Paul has done nothing worthy of death, and in the same chapter Festus and Agrippa agree that Paul might well have been released had he not appealed to Caesar. Luke was writing in the days when Christians were disliked and persecuted, and he told his story in such a way as to show that the Roman magistrates had always been perfectly fair to Christianity and that they had never regarded the Christians as evil men. In fact, the very interesting suggestion has been made that Acts is nothing other than the brief which was prepared for Paul's defence when he stood his trial before the Roman Emperor.

(ii) One of Luke's aims was to show that Christianity was a universal religion for all men of every country. This was one of the things that the Jews found it hard to grasp and to understand. They had the idea that they were God's chosen people and they were sure that God had no use for any other nation. Luke sets out to prove that that is not so. He shows Philip preaching to the Samaritans ; he shows Stephen making Christianity a universal thing and being killed for it ; he shows Peter accepting Cornelius into the Church ; he shows the Christians preaching to the Gentiles at Antioch ; he shows Paul travelling far and wide winning men of all kinds for Christ ; and in Acts 15 he shows the Church making the great decision to accept the Gentiles on equal terms with the Jews. Undoubtedly Luke wished to show that Christianity was a religion which knew no bounds.

(iii) But these were merely secondary aims. Luke's

great aim is set out in the words of the Risen Christ in
I : 8, " Ye shall be witnesses unto me both in Jerusalem
and in all Judaea and in Samaria and unto the uttermost
parts of the earth." Luke's great aim was to show the
expansion of Christianity, to show how that religion which
began in a little corner of Palestine had in little more than
thirty years reached Rome. C. H. Turner has pointed
out how Acts falls into six panels, each one ending with
what might be called a progress report. The six panels
are as follows :—

(a) I : I—6 : 7 ; this tells of the Church at Jerusalem
and the preaching of Peter ; and it finishes with
the summary, " The word of God was increasing,
and the number of the disciples in Jerusalem was
being greatly multiplied ; and a large number of
priests were becoming obedient to the faith."

(b) 6 : 8—9 : 31 ; this describes the spread of Christianity through Palestine and the martyrdom of
Stephen, which was followed by the preaching in
Samaria. It ends with the summary, " The Church
then through all Galilee was having peace and
being built up and, walking in the fear of the Lord,
was being multiplied."

(c) 9 : 32—12 : 24 ; this includes the conversion of
Paul, the extension of the Church to Antioch, and
the reception of Cornelius, the Gentile, into the
Church by Peter. Its summary is, " And the word
of God was increasing and being multiplied."

(d) 12 : 25—16 : 5 ; this tells of the extension of the
Church through Asia Minor and the preaching tour
of Galatia. It ends, " The Churches then were being
confirmed in the faith and were abounding more in
number daily."

(e) 16 : 6—19 : 20 ; this relates the extension of the
Church to Europe and the work of Paul in great
Gentile cities like Corinth and Ephesus. Its summary
runs, " So mightily was the word of God increasing
and prevailing."

(f) 19 : 21—28 : 31 ; this tells of the arrival of Paul in Rome and his imprisonment there. It ends with the picture of Paul " proclaiming the Kingdom of God and teaching the things concerning the Lord Jesus Christ with all boldness and unhindered."

This plan of Acts explains the very fact about Acts which at first sight is most puzzling. Why does Acts finish where it does ? It finishes with Paul in prison awaiting judgment. We would so much have liked to know what happened to Paul, but the end is wrapped in mystery. But Luke stopped there because his purpose was accomplished. He has shown how Christianity began in Jerusalem and swept across the world until it reached the great city of Rome. A great New Testament scholar has said that the title of Acts might be, " How they brought the Good News from Jerusalem to Rome." Luke's aim was to set before men the well-nigh miraculous spread of the Gospel, and he laid down his pen when he had shown Christianity established in the capital of the world.

Luke's Sources

Luke was an historian, and the source from which an historian draws his information is all important. Where then did Luke get his facts ? In this connection Acts falls into two parts.

(i) There are the first fifteen chapters. Of the events therein described Luke had no personal knowledge. He very likely had access to two sources. (a) There were the records of the local Churches. They may never have been set down in writing but the Churches had their stories. In this section we can distinguish three records. There is the record of the *Jerusalem Church* which we find in chapters I to 5 and in chapters 15 and 16. There is the record of *the Church at Caesarea* which covers 8 : 26-40 and 9 : 31— 10 : 48. There is the record of the *Church at Antioch* which includes II : 19-30 and 12 : 25—14 : 28 ; (b) Still further, no doubt tales and stories would accumulate round the great figures of the Church and very likely there were cycles of stories which were the Acts of Peter, the Acts of John, the Acts of Philip and the Acts of Stephen. Beyond a doubt Luke's friendship with Paul would bring him into touch with all the great men of all the Churches and all their records and stories would be at his disposal.

(ii) There are chapters 16 to 28. Of much of this section Luke had personal first hand knowledge. When we read Acts carefully we notice a strange thing. In certain passages Luke writes, " They did this," and " they did that." And then all of a sudden he changes to " we did this," and " we did that." The " we " passages are as follows— Acts 16 : 10-17 ; 20 : 5-16 ; 21 : 1-18 ; 27 : 1—28 : 16. On all these occasions Luke must have been present. He must have kept a travel diary and in these passages we have an eye-witness account. As for the times when he was not present, many were the hours he must have spent in prison with Paul and many were the stories Paul must have told him. There can have been no great figure Luke did not know and in every case he must have got his story from someone who was there.

When we read Acts we may be quite sure that no historian ever had better sources and no historian ever used his sources more accurately and more honestly.

THE ACTS OF THE APOSTLES

POWER TO GO ON

Acts I : I-5

> My Dear Theophilus, I have already given you an
> account of all the things that Jesus began to do and to
> teach, right up to the day when He was taken up to
> heaven, after He had, through the Holy Spirit, given
> His instructions to the apostles whom He had chosen.
> In the days that followed His sufferings He also showed
> Himself living to them by many proofs, for He was seen
> by them on various occasions throughout a period of
> forty days ; and He spoke to them about the Kingdom
> of God. While He was staying with them He told them
> not to go away from Jerusalem but to wait for the
> Father's promise, " which," He said, " I told you about;
> for I told you that John baptized with water but you
> will be baptized with the Holy Spirit before many days
> have passed."

IN two senses the Book of Acts is the second chapter of a
continued story. First, it is literally the second volume
which Luke had sent to Theophilus. In the first volume,
which was his Gospel, Luke had told the story of the life of
Jesus upon earth, and now he goes on to tell the story of the
Christian Church. But, second, Acts is the second volume
of a story which has no end. The Gospel was only the story
of what Jesus *began* to do and to teach. Jesus' earthly life
was only the beginning of an activity which knows no end.
There are different kinds of immortality. There is an
immortality of fame. In *Henry the Fifth* Shakespeare puts
into the king's mouth that speech which promises an
immortal memory if the Battle of Agincourt is won.

> This story shall the good man tell his son ;
> And Crispin Crispian shall ne'er go by,
> From this day to the ending of the world,
> But we in it shall be remembered.

Beyond a doubt Jesus did win such an immortality, for
His name will never be forgotten. There is an *immortality
of influence.* Some men leave an influence and an

I

effect in the world which cannot die. Sir Francis Drake was the greatest of English sailors, and to this day the Royal Naval Barracks at Plymouth is called *H.M.S. Drake* so that there may always be sailors armed with " that crested and prevailing name." Beyond a doubt Jesus did win an immortality of influence for His effect upon the world and the life of men cannot die. But, above all, there is an *immortality of presence and of power.* Jesus did not only leave an immortal name and influence ; He is still alive and still active and still powerful. He is not the one who *was* ; He is the one who *is* and His life still goes on.

In one sense it is the whole lesson of the Book of Acts that that life of Jesus goes on *in His Church.* Dr. John Foster tells how an inquirer from Hinduism came to an Indian Bishop. All unaided he had read the New Testament, and the story had fascinated him and Christ had laid His spell upon him. " Then he read on . . . and felt he had entered into a new world. In the gospels it was Jesus, His works and His suffering. In the Acts . . . what the disciples did and thought and taught had taken the place that Christ had occupied. The Church continued where Jesus had left off at His death. ' Therefore,' said this man to me, ' I must belong to *the Church that carries on the life of Christ.* ' " The Book of Acts tells of the Church that carries on the life of Christ.

Now this passage tells us how the Church was empowered to do that. It was empowered to do so by the work of the Holy Spirit. We often call the Holy Spirit *the Comforter.* That word goes back to Wycliff ; but in Wycliff's day it had a different meaning. It comes from the Latin *fortis,* which means *brave* ; and the Comforter is the one who fills men with courage and with strength. In the Book of Acts, and indeed all through the New Testament, it is very difficult to draw a line between the work of the Spirit and the work of the Risen Christ ; and indeed we do not need to do so, for the coming of the Spirit is the fulfilment of the promise of Jesus, " Lo, I am with you alway even unto the end of the world." (Matthew 28 : 20). Let us note one other thing. The apostles were enjoined to *wait* on the coming of the Spirit. We would gain more power and courage and peace if we learned to wait. In the business of life we need to learn to be still. " They that wait upon the Lord shall renew their strength." (Isaiah 40 : 31). Amidst life's surging activity there must be room for a wise passiveness. Amidst all the striving there must be time to receive.

THE KINGDOM AND ITS WITNESSES

Acts I : 6-8

> So when they had met together they asked Him, " Lord, are you going to restore the kingdom of Israel at this time ? " But He said to them, " It is not yours to know the times and the seasons which the Father has appointed by His own authority. But when the Holy Spirit has come upon you, you will receive power ; and you will be my witnesses both in Jerusalem and in all Judaea and in Samaria and to the farthest bounds of the earth."

THROUGHOUT all His ministry Jesus laboured under one great disadvantage. The centre of His message was the Kingdom of God. (Mark I : 14). But the trouble was that He meant one thing by the Kingdom and those who listened to Him meant quite another. The Jews were always vividly conscious of being God's chosen people. They took that to mean that they were inevitably destined for special honour and privilege and for world-wide dominion. The whole course of their history proved that humanly speaking that could never be. Palestine was a little country not more than 120 miles long by 40 miles wide. It had its days of independence but it had become subject in turn to the Babylonians, the Persians, the Greeks and the Romans. So the Jews began to look forward to a day when God would break directly into human history, and when He by His might would do what they themselves could never do. They looked for a day when by divine intervention the world sovereignty they dreamed of would be theirs. They conceived of the Kingdom in political terms. How did Jesus conceive of it ? Let us look at the Lord's Prayer. In it there are two petitions side by side. " Thy Kingdom come ; Thy will be done in earth as it is in heaven." Now, it is characteristic of Hebrew style, as any verse of the Psalms will show, to say things in two parallel forms, the second of which repeats or amplifies the first. That is what these two petitions do. The second of the two petitions is a definition of the first ; and, therefore, we see that, by the Kingdom, Jesus meant a society upon earth where God's will would be as perfectly done as it is in heaven. Because of that very fact it would be a Kingdom founded on love and not on power.

To attain to that men needed the Holy Spirit. Twice already Luke has talked about waiting for the coming of the Spirit. We are not to think that the Spirit came into existence now for the first time. It is quite possible for a power always to exist but for men to experience or take it at some given moment. For instance, men did not invent atomic power. It always existed ; but only in our time have men tapped it and experienced it. So God is eternally Father, Son and Holy Spirit, but there came to men a special time when they experienced to the full that power which had always been present.

The power of the Spirit was going to make them Christ's witnesses. That witness was to operate in an ever-extending series of concentric circles, first in Jerusalem, then throughout Judaea ; then Samaria, the semi-Jewish state, would be a kind of bridge leading out into the heathen world ; and finally this witness was to go out to the ends of the earth.

Let us note certain things about this Christian witness. First, a witness is a man who says I know this is true. In a court of law a man cannot give in evidence a carried story ; it must be his own personal experience. There was a time when John Bunyan was not quite sure. What worried him was that the Jews think their religion the best religion ; the Mohammedans think their religion the best religion. What if Christianity be but a *think-so* too ? A witness does not say, " I think so " ; he says " I know."

Second, the real witness is not the witness of words but of deeds. When H. M. Stanley had discovered David Livingstone in Central Africa, and when he had spent some time with him, he said, " If I had been with him any longer I would have been compelled to be a Christian and he never spoke to me about it at all." The sheer weight of the witness of the man's life was irresistible.

Third, it is one of the most suggestive facts that in Greek the word for *witness* and the word for *martyr* is the same word (*martus*). A witness had to be ready to become a martyr. To be a witness means to be loyal no matter what the cost.

THE GLORY OF DEPARTURE AND THE GLORY OF RETURN

Acts I : 9-11

> When He had said these things, while they were watching, He was taken up and a cloud received Him and He passed from their sight. While they were gazing into heaven, as He went upon His way, behold, two men in white garments stood beside them ; and they said to them, " Men of Galilee, why are you standing looking up into heaven ? This Jesus who has been taken up into heaven from you will come again in the same way as you have seen Him go to heaven."

THIS short passage leaves us face to face with two of the most difficult conceptions in the New Testament. First, it tells us the story of the Ascension. Only Luke tells us this story, and he has already related it in his gospel. (Luke 24 : 50-53). Now the Ascension is not a conception of which we have any cause to be hesitant or doubtful. For two reasons the Ascension was an absolute necessity. First, it was necessary that there should be one final moment when Jesus did go back to the glory which was His. The forty days of the resurrection appearances had passed. Clearly that was a time which was unique and could not go on forever. Now equally clearly the end to that period had to be definite. There would have been something quite wrong if the resurrection appearances had just slowly faded out, if the whole thing, to use a colloquial phrase, had simply petered out. It was necessary that as Jesus in a moment of time had arrived in the world in a moment of time He should leave it. For the second reason we must transport ourselves in imagination back to the time when this happened. It is nowadays correct to say that we do not regard heaven as some local place beyond the sky ; we regard heaven as a state of blessedness when we will be forever and inseparably with God. But all this happened close on two thousand years ago ; and every man, even the wisest man, in those days still thought of this as a flat earth with a place called heaven beyond the sky. It therefore follows that if Jesus was to give His followers unanswerable proof that He had returned to His glory, the Ascension was absolutely necessary. It was the one possible proof that Jesus had returned to glory. But we must note one thing. When Luke tells of this in his gospel he adds something. He says, " They returned to Jerusalem with great joy." (Luke 24 : 52). In spite of the Ascension, or maybe, because of it, the disciples were quite sure that Jesus was not gone from them, but that He was with them forever.

But second, this passage brings us face to face with the Second Coming. About the Second Coming we must remember two things. First, to speculate when it will happen and how it will happen is both foolish and useless, because Jesus Himself said that not even He knew the day and the hour when the Son of Man would come. (Mark 13 : 32). There is something almost blasphemous in speculating about that which was hidden from even Christ Himself. Second, the essential teaching of Christianity is that God has a plan for man and the world. We are bound to believe that history is not a haphazard conglomeration of chance events which are going nowhere. We are bound to believe that the world is going somewhere, that there is some divine far off event to which the whole creation moves. And we are bound to believe that when that consummation comes Jesus Christ will indeed be Judge and Lord of all. The Second Coming is not a matter for speculation and for an illegitimate curiosity. It is a summons to strive for the coming of that day and to make ourselves ready for it when it comes.

THE FATE OF THE TRAITOR

Acts I : I2-20

Then they made their way back to Jerusalem from the hill which is called the Mount of Olives, which is near Jerusalem, about half a mile away. When they came in, they went up to the upper room where they were staying ; Peter and John and James and Andrew, Philip and Thomas, Bartholomew and Matthew, James the son of Alphaeus and Simon the Zealot and Judas the son of James were there. All of them with one united heart persevered in prayer, together with certain women and with Mary, Jesus' mother and with His brothers.

And in these days Peter stood up amongst the brethren and said—the number of people who were together was about one hundred and twenty—"Brethren, the scripture had to be fulfilled, which the Holy Spirit foretold through the mouth of David about Judas who was guide to those who arrested Jesus, because he was one of our number and had received his allotted part in our service. (This man bought a piece of ground with the proceeds of his wicked deed ; and he fell headlong and burst asunder and his bowels gushed out. This became a well-known fact to all those who lived in Jerusalem so that the piece of ground was called in their language Akeldama, which means the place of blood.) For it stands written in the Book of Psalms, ' Let the place where he lodged be desolate and let no one stay in it.' And, ' Let another receive his office.' "

BEFORE we come to the fate of the traitor Judas there are certain things we may notice in this passage. For the Jew the Sabbath was entirely a day of rest when all work was absolutely forbidden. On the Sabbath a journey was limited to 2,000 cubits, and that distance was called a Sabbath day's journey. A cubit was eighteen inches ; so a Sabbath day's journey was rather more than half a mile.

It is very interesting to note that Jesus' brothers are here with the company of the disciples. During Jesus' lifetime they had been amongst His opponents (Mark 3 : 21). It may well be that for them, as for so many others, the death of Jesus opened their eyes and stabbed their hearts as even His life could not do.

We are told that the number of the disciples was about 120. That is one of the most uplifting things in the New Testament. There were only 120 men who were pledged to Christ. It is very unlikely that any of them had ever been outside the narrow confines of Palestine in his life. To take the figures for Palestine alone, there were about 4,000,000 Jews in Palestine. That is fewer than 1 in 30,000 were Christians. On the same basis it would mean that it was as if there were about 300 Christians in the whole of Glasgow or about 12 in Edinburgh ; and these 120 simple men were told to go out and to evangelise a whole world. If ever anything began from small beginnings the Christian Church did. It may well be that we are the only Christians in the shop, the factory, the office in which we work, in the circle amidst which we move. These men gallantly faced their task and so must we, and it may well be that we too will be the small beginning from which the Kingdom in our sphere will spread.

But the great interest of this passage is the fate of Judas the traitor. What exactly the Greek of this passage means is uncertain, but in Matthew's account (Matthew 27 : 3-5) we are left in no doubt that Judas committed suicide. It must always be a matter of wonder why Judas betrayed Jesus. Various suggestions have been put forward.

(i) It has been suggested that *Iscariot* means *man of Kerioth*. If it does, Judas was the only non-Galilaean in the apostolic band. It may be from the beginning that he felt himself the odd man out and grew so embittered that he did this terrible thing.

(ii) It may be that Judas turned king's evidence to save his own skin and then saw the awful thing that he had done.

(iii) It may be that he did it simply because he was greedy for money. If he did, it was the most dreadful bargain in history, for he sold his Lord for thirty pieces of silver which was less than £4.

(iv) It may be that Judas came to hate Jesus. From others he could disguise his own black heart ; but the eyes of Jesus could strip away the disguises and penetrate like X-rays to the inmost recesses of his being. And it may be that in the end he was driven to destroy the one who knew him for what he was.

(v) It may be that Iscariot is a form of a Greek word which means a dagger bearer. The dagger bearers were a band of violent nationalists who were prepared to undertake assassination and murder in a campaign to set Palestine free. Perhaps Judas saw in Jesus with His wonderful powers the very person who could lead the nationalists to triumph ; and then when he saw that Jesus refused the way of power he turned against Him, and in his bitter disappointment betrayed Him.

(vi) But likeliest of all, it may well be that Judas never meant Jesus to die. He may well have betrayed Jesus with the intention of forcing Jesus' hand. He may have sought to put Jesus into a position in which, if He was to save His own life, He would be bound to use His power, and where He would be forced to act against the Romans. If that be so, Judas had the tragic experience of seeing his plan go desperately wrong ; and in his bitter remorse he committed suicide.

However it may be, Judas goes down to history as the blackest name among men. There can never be any peace for the man who betrays Christ, and who is false to his Lord.

THE QUALIFICATIONS OF AN APOSTLE

Acts I : 21-26

> " So then, of the men who were with us during all the time our Lord went in and out amongst us, beginning from the baptism of John until the day on which He was taken up from us—of these we must choose one to be a witness of the Resurrection along with us." So they selected two, Joseph, who was called Barsabbas, whose surname was Justus, and Matthias. Then they prayed and said, " O Lord, who knowest the hearts of all, do Thou show us which of these two Thou hast chosen to take his place in this service and in the apostleship, from which Judas fell away and went to his own place." So they made them draw lots and the lot fell on Matthias, and he was elected to be along with the eleven apostles.

FIRST, we may look briefly at the method of choosing some-one to take Judas' place in the number of the apostles. It may seem to us strange that the method was that of casting lots. But amongst the Jews it was the natural thing to do, because all the offices and duties in the Temple were settled by lot. The normal way of doing it was that the names of the candidates were written on stones ; the stones were then put into a vessel and the vessel was shaken until one stone fell out ; and he whose name was on the first stone to fall out was elected to office.

But the great fact about this passage is that it gives us two supremely important truths.

First, it tells us the *function of an apostle*. The function of an apostle was to be a witness to the Resurrection. The real mark of a Christian is not that he knows about Jesus, but that he knows Jesus. The one basic mistake in Christianity is to regard Jesus as someone who lived and died, and whose life we study and whose story we read. Jesus is not a figure in a book. He is a living presence, and the Christian is the man whose whole life is a witness to the fact that he knows and has met the Risen Lord.

Second, it tells us the *qualification of an apostle*. The qualification of an apostle was that he had companied with Jesus. The real Christian is the man who lives day by day with Jesus. It was said of John Brown, of Haddington, the great preacher, that often when he preached he paused as if listening for a voice. Jerome K. Jerome tells of an old cobbler who, on the coldest day, left the door of his shop open, and on being asked why, replied, " So that *He* can come in if He is passing by." We often speak about what would happen if Jesus were here and how differently we would live if He were in our homes and at our work. Lady Acland tells how once her little daughter had a spasm of temper. After the storm she and the daughter were sitting on the stairs making things up again and the little girl said, " I wish Jesus would come and stay in our house all the time." But the point and the fact is that Jesus *is* here ; and the real Christian, the real apostle, is the man who still lives all his life with Christ.

THE DAY OF PENTECOST

We may never know precisely what happened on the Day of Pentecost, but we do know that it was one of the supremely great days of the Christian Church, for on that day the Holy Spirit came to the Christian Church in a very special way.

The Book of Acts has been called the Gospel of the Holy Spirit ; if ever a doctrine needed to be re-discovered it is the doctrine of the Holy Spirit ; so before we turn to the detailed consideration of the second chapter of Acts let us take a general view of what Acts has to say and teach about the Holy Spirit.

The Coming of the Spirit.

It is perhaps unfortunate that we so often speak of the events at Pentecost as the coming of the Holy Spirit.

(Acts 20 : 28). All the members of the early Church lived in the Spirit as they lived in the very air which they breathed.

For still another thing, *the Spirit was the source of day to day courage and power.* The disciples were to receive power when the Spirit had come (Acts 1 : 8) ; Peter's courage and eloquence before the Sanhedrin are the result of the activity of the Spirit (Acts 4 : 31) ; in Cyprus Paul's conquest of Elymas is the work of the Spirit (Acts 13 : 9). The Christian courage to meet the dangerous situation ; the Christian power to cope with life more than adequately ; the Christian eloquence when eloquence was needed ; the Christian joy which was independent of circumstances are all alike ascribed to the work of the Spirit.

For one last thing, in Acts 5 : 32 there is a very suggestive saying. That verse speaks of the Spirit, " whom God has given to those who obey Him." This has in it the great truth that *the measure of the Spirit which a man can possess is conditioned by the kind of man he is.* It means that the man who is honestly trying to do the will of God will experience more and more of the wonder of the Spirit. It means that the living of the Christian life brings with it its own power.

In the first thirteen chapters of Acts there are more than forty references to the Holy Spirit. The early Church was a Spirit-filled Church and precisely therein lay its power.

Now let us turn to study the second chapter of Acts, which tells of the coming of the Spirit.

THE BREATH OF GOD

Acts 2 : 1-13

> So when the day of Pentecost came round, they were all together in one place ; and all of a sudden there came from heaven a sound like that of a violent, rushing wind and it filled the whole house where

The Feast itself had two main significances. (i) It had an *historical* significance. It commemorated the giving of the Law to Moses on Mount Sinai. (ii) It had an agricultural significance. At the Passover the first omer of barley of the crop was offered to God ; and at Pentecost two loaves were offered in gratitude for the completed and the ingathered harvest. It had one other unique characteristic. The law laid it down that on that day no servile work should be done (Leviticus 23 : 21 ; Numbers 28 : 26). So it was a holiday for all men, and the crowds on the streets would be greater than ever.

What happened at Pentecost we really do not know. Certain it is that the disciples had an experience of the power of the Spirit flooding their beings such as they never had before. We must remember that for this part of Acts Luke was not an eye-witness and that he was passing on a story which he must have heard. He tells the story as if the disciples suddenly acquired the gift of speaking in *foreign* languages. For two reasons that is not likely. (i) There was in the early Church a phenomenon which has never completely passed away. It was called *speaking with tongues* (cp. Acts 10 : 46 ; 19 : 6). The main passage which describes it is I Corinthians 14. What happened was that someone, in an ecstasy, began to pour out a flood of unintelligible sounds in no known language. That was supposed to be directly inspired by the Spirit of God. Strange as it may sound to us, it was a gift greatly coveted. Paul did not greatly approve of it, because it seemed to him far to be preferred that a message should be given in a language that could be understood. He in fact said that if a stranger came in he might well think he had arrived in a congregation of madmen (I Corinthians 14 : 23). Now that precisely fits Acts 2 : 13. Men speaking in tongues would appear to be drunk to someone who did not know the phenomenon. On these grounds it is much more likely that this passage refers to that strange, yet coveted, gift, of speaking with tongues. (ii) To speak in foreign languages was unnecessary. The passage says that the crowd was made up of Jews (verse 5) and proselytes (verse 10). Proselytes were Gentiles who had grown tired of the multitude of heathen gods, and who had grown weary of heathen immorality and laxity and who had come to the Synagogues to learn of the one God and the clean way of life, and who had accepted the Jewish religion and the Jewish way of life. Now for a crowd like that at most two languages were necessary. Almost all Jews spoke Aramaic ; and even if they were Jews of the Dispersion from a foreign land, they would speak that language which almost everyone in the world spoke at that time— Greek. Greek had become a world language which everyone spoke in addition to his own tongue. In point of fact Aramaic and Greek, which the disciples must anyhow have spoken, would be quite sufficient. It seems by far most likely that Luke, a Gentile, had confused speaking with tongues with speaking with *foreign* tongues. What happened was that for the first time in their lives this motley mob was hearing the word of God in a way that struck straight home to their hearts and that they could understand. The power of the Spirit was such that it had given these simple disciples a message and an utterance that could reach every heart.

THE FIRST CHRISTIAN PREACHING

Acts 2 : 14-42 is one of the most interesting passages in the whole New Testament, because it is an account of the first Christian sermon ever preached. Now in the early Church there were four different kinds of preaching. (i) There was what is called *kerugma*. *Kerugma* literally means *a herald's announcement* and is the plain statement of the facts of the Christian message, about which, as the early preachers saw it, there can be no argument and of which there can be no denial. (ii) There was what is called *didache*. *Didache* literally means *teaching* and elucidated and worked out the meanings, the significances, the implications of the facts which have been proclaimed. To put it in modern and colloquial terms—suppose a preacher had stated the unanswerable facts, and suppose a listener asked, " So what ? "—*didache* is the answer to that question. (iii) There was what is called *paraklesis* which literally means *exhortation*. This kind of preaching urged upon men the duty and the obligation of fitting their lives to match the *kerugma* and the *didache* which had just been given. (iv) There was what was called *homilia* which means the treatment of any subject or department of life in light of the Christian message. Fully rounded preaching has something of all four elements. There is the plain proclamation of the facts of the Christian gospel ; the explanation of the meaning and the relevance of these facts ; the exhortation to fit life to them ; and the treatment of all the activities of life in the light of the Christian message.

Now in the Book of Acts we shall meet mainly with *kerugma* because the Book of Acts tells of the proclamation of the facts of the gospel to those who had never heard them before. This *kerugma* follows a pattern which repeats itself over and over again all over the New Testament.

(i) There is the proof that Jesus, and all that happened to Jesus, is the fulfilment of Old Testament prophecy. In modern times less and less stress has been laid on the fulfilment of prophecy. We have come to see that the prophets were not nearly so much *fore-tellers* of events to come as they were *forth-tellers* of God's truth to men. But this stress of early preaching on prophecy conserves and lays down one great truth. It lays down the great truth that history is not haphazard ; that it is not a knotless thread ; but that there is a meaning and sense and a moral law at work in the universe. To believe in the possibility of prophecy is to believe that God is in control and that He is working out His purposes.

(ii) In Jesus the Messiah has come, the Messianic prophecies are fulfilled and the New Age has dawned.

The early Church had a tremendous sense that Jesus **was** the hinge of all history ; that with His coming, eternity had invaded time and God had entered the human arena ; and that, therefore, life and the world could never be the same again. With the coming of Jesus something crucial, unrepeatable, all-affecting had emerged.

(iii) The early preaching then went on to state that Jesus had been born of the line of David, that He had taught and worked miracles, that He had been crucified, that He had been raised from the dead and was now at the right hand of God. The early Church was quite sure that the whole Christian religion had an historical basis, that it was based on the earthly life of Christ, and that the story of that life must be told. But it was also certain that that earthly life and death were not the end, but that after them there came the Resurrection. The basis was the historical facts, but these historical facts were not the sum total of everything. Jesus was to them not someone about whom they read or to the story of whom they listened ; He was someone whom they met and knew and experienced. He was not a figure in a book, one who had lived and died ; He was a living presence, alive for evermore.

(iv) The early preachers went on to insist that Jesus would return again in glory to establish His Kingdom upon earth. In other words, the early Church believed intensely and passionately in the Second Coming. Again that is a doctrine which has to some extent passed out of modern preaching. But at basis it does conserve one great truth—the truth that history is going somewhere, that some day, some time, there will be a consummation ; and that a man is therefore in the way, or on the way.

(v) The preaching finished with the statement that in Jesus alone is salvation, that he who believes on Him will receive the Holy Spirit, and that he who will not believe is destined for terrible things. That is to say, it finished with both a *promise* and a *threat*. It is exactly like that voice which Bunyan heard as if at his very shoulder demanding, " Wilt thou leave thy sins and go to heaven, or wilt thou have thy sins and go to hell ? "

If we read through Peter's sermon now as a whole we will see how these five strands are woven into it.

GOD'S DAY HAS COME

Acts 2 : 14-21

> But Peter stood up with the eleven and raised his voice and said to them, " You who are Jews and you who are staying in Jerusalem, let this be known to you and listen to my words. These men are not, as you suppose, drunk ; for it is only nine o'clock in the morning. But this is what was spoken by the prophet Joel, ' It will be in the last days, says God, that I will pour out from my Spirit upon all men, and your sons and your daughters will prophesy and your young men will see visions and your old men will dream dreams. And I will pour out from my Spirit upon my men servants and my maid servants in these days and they will prophesy. I will send wonders in the heaven above and signs upon the earth below, blood and fire and vapour of smoke. The sun will be changed into darkness and the moon into blood before there comes the great and famous day of the Lord. And it shall be that all whosoever shall call upon the name of the Lord shall be saved.' "

IN verse 15 Peter insists that these men cannot be drunk because it is the *third hour*. The Jewish day ran from 6 a.m. until 6 p.m., and, therefore, the third hour is nine o'clock in the morning.

The whole passage brings us face to face with one of the basic and dominant conceptions of both the Old and the New Testaments—the conception of *The Day of the Lord*. There is much both in the Old and in the New Testaments which is not fully intelligible unless we know the basic principles underlying that conception. The Jews never lost the conviction that they were God's chosen people. They interpreted that status to mean that they were chosen for special honour and special privilege among the nations. They were always a small nation. History had been for them one long disaster. It was clear to them that by human means they would never reach the status they deserved as the chosen people. So, bit by bit, they reached the conclusion that what man could not do God must do. So they began to look forward to a day when God would intervene directly in history and exalt them to the honour they dreamed of. The day of that intervention was *The Day of the Lord*. They divided all time into two ages. There was *The Present Age* which was utterly evil and doomed to destruction ; there was *The Age to Come* which would be the golden age of God. Between the two there was to be *The Day of the Lord* and it was to be the terrible birth pangs of the new age. It would come suddenly like a thief in the night ; it would be a day when the world would be shaken to its very foundations, and the universe itself would come crashing into disintegration ; it would be a day of judgment and of terror. All over the prophetic books of the Old Testament, and in much of the New Testament, are descriptions of that Day. Typical passages are Isaiah 2 : 12 ; 13 : 6ff ; Amos 5 : 18 ; Zephaniah 1 : 7 ; Joel 2 ; 1 Thessalonians 5 : 2ff ; 2 Peter 3 : 10. Here Peter is saying to these Jews—" For generations you have dreamed of the Day of God, the Day when God would break into history. Now, in Jesus, that Day has come." Behind all the outworn imagery there stands the one great truth—In Jesus, God in person arrived on the scene of human history.

LORD AND CHRIST

Acts 2 : 22-36

" Men of Israel, listen to these words. Jesus of Nazareth, a man approved by God to you by deeds of power and wonders and signs, which God, among you, did through Him, as you yourselves know—this man, delivered up by the fore-ordained knowledge and counsel of

God, you took and crucified by the hand of wicked men. But God raised Him up and loosed the pains of death because it was impossible that He should be held subject by it. For David says in regard to Him, ' Always I foresaw the Lord before me, because He is at my right hand so that I should not be shaken. Because of this my heart has rejoiced and my tongue has exulted, and, furthermore, my flesh shall dwell in hope, because Thou wilt not leave my soul in the land of the dead, nor wilt Thou suffer Thy Holy One to see corruption. Thou hast made known to me the ways of life. Thou shalt make me full of joy with Thy countenance.' Brethren, I can speak to you freely about the patriarch David, that he is both dead and buried and his memorial is amongst us to this day. Thus he was a prophet ; and because he knew that God had sworn an oath to him, that one of his descendants should sit upon his throne, he spoke with foresight about the resurrection of the Christ, that He would neither be left in the world of the dead, nor would His flesh see corruption. This Jesus God raised up and all of us are His witnesses. So then when He had been exalted to the right hand of God He received the promise of the Holy Spirit from the Father and poured out this which you see and hear. For David did not ascend up into heaven, and yet he says, ' The Lord said to my Lord, sit upon my right hand until I make Thine enemies Thy footstool for Thy feet.' So then let all the house of Israel certainly know that God has made this Jesus whom you crucified Lord and Christ.''

HERE is a passage which is full of the very essence of the thought of the early preachers.

(i) It insists that the Cross was no accident. It belonged to the eternal plan of God (verse 23). Over and over again Acts states that the Cross is in the eternal plan of God (cp. 3 : 18 ; 4 : 28 ; 13 : 29). The thought of Acts safeguards us from two serious errors in our thinking about the death of Jesus. (a) The Cross is not a kind of emergency measure flung out by God when everything else had failed. It is part of the very life of God. (b) We must never think that anything Jesus did changed the attitude of God to men. We must never set a gentle loving Jesus over against an angry, vengeful God. It was *by God* Jesus was sent. It was God who planned the coming of Jesus into the world. We may put it this way, the Cross was a window in time to allow us to see the suffering love which is eternally in the heart of God.

(ii) Acts insists that, though that is so, it in no way lessens the crime of those who crucified Jesus. Every mention of the crucifixion in Acts is instinct with a feeling of shuddering horror at the crime men committed in it (cp. Acts 2 : 23 ; 3 : 13 ; 4 : 10 ; 5 : 30). Apart from anything else, the crucifixion is the greatest crime in history. It shows supremely what sin can do, that sin can take the loveliest life the world ever saw and seek to break it on a cross.

(iii) Acts is out to prove that the sufferings and the death of Christ were the fulfilment of prophecy. The earliest preachers had to do that. To the Jew the idea of a crucified Messiah was incredible. Their law said, " Cursed be everyone who hangs on a tree " (Deuteronomy 21 : 23). To the orthodox Jew the Cross was the one fact which made it completely impossible that Jesus could be the Messiah. The early preachers answered, " If you would only read your scriptures rightly you would see that all was foretold."

(iv) Acts stresses the Resurrection as the final proof that Jesus was indeed God's Chosen One. Acts has been called The Gospel of the Resurrection. To the early Church the Resurrection was all-important. We must remember this—*without the Resurrection there would have been no Christian Church at all*. When the disciples preached the centrality of the Resurrection they were arguing from experience. After the Cross they were bewildered, broken men, with their dream gone and their lives shattered. It was the Resurrection which changed all that and turned hopeless men into men pulsating with confidence, and cowards into heroes. It is one of the tragedies of the

Church that so often the preaching of the Resurrection is confined to Easter time. Every Sunday is the Lord's Day ; every Lord's Day should be kept as Resurrection day. In the Eastern Church on Easter day, if two people meet, one says, " The Lord is risen " ; and the other answers, " He is risen indeed ! " A Christian is a man who never forgets that he lives and walks with a Risen Lord.

SAVE YOURSELVES

Acts 2 : 37-41

> When they heard this, they were pierced to the heart, and they said to Peter and to the other apostles, " Brethren, what are we to do ? " Peter said to them, " Repent, and let each of you be baptized in the name of Jesus Christ so that your sins may be forgiven ; and you will receive the gift of the Holy Spirit, for this promise is to you and to your children and to all who are afar off, to all those whom the Lord your God invites." With many other words he gave his witness and he urged them, " Save yourselves from this crooked generation." So they accepted his word and were baptized and on that day there were added to them about three thousand people.

(i) FIRST, this passage shows us with crystal clarity the effect of the Cross. When men were shown just what they had done in crucifying Jesus their hearts were broken. " I," said Jesus, " if I be lifted up from the earth will draw all men unto Me " (John 12 : 32). If man's sin was responsible for the crucifying of Jesus then *our* sin was responsible for it. Every man has had a hand in that crime. It is told that once a missionary told the story of Jesus in an Indian village. Afterwards he showed the life of Christ in lantern slides thrown against the white-washed wall of a house. Suddenly when the slide of the Cross appeared on the wall one man rose from the audience and ran forward. " Come down from that Cross, Son of God," he cried. " I, not you, should be hanging there."

The Cross, when we understand what happened there, cannot do other than pierce the heart.

(ii) That experience demands a reaction from men. " Repent," said Peter, " first and foremost." Now what does repentance mean ? The word originally meant an *afterthought,* a second thought. Often a second thought shows that the first thought was wrong ; and so the word came to mean *a change of mind* ; but, if a man is an honest man, a change of mind demands *a change of action.* Repentance must involve both change of mind and change of action. A man may change his mind and come to see that his actions were wrong, but he may be so much in love with his old ways that he does not change his ways. A man may change his ways but his mind may remain exactly the same. He may only change because of fear or because of prudential motives ; his heart still loves the old ways and, if the chance comes, he will relapse into them. True repentance involves a change of mind *and* a change of action.

(iii) When repentance comes something happens *to the past.* There is *remission of sins.* There is God's forgiveness for that which lies behind. Let us be quite clear that the *consequences* of sins are not wiped out. Not even God can do that. When we sin we may well do something to ourselves and to others which cannot be undone. Let us look at it this way. When we were young and had done something bad there was an invisible barrier between us and our parents. But when we went and said we were sorry, and when we felt our mother's arms about us again, the old relationship was restored and we were right with her again. Forgiveness does not abolish the consequences of what we have done but it puts us right with God again. The estrangement and the fear are gone and we are at peace with God.

(iv) When repentance comes something happens *for the future.* We receive *the gift of the Holy Spirit.* Even if we repent, how are we to avoid making the same mistakes over and over again ? There comes into our lives the power which is not our power, the power of the Holy Spirit, and in that power we can win the battles we never thought to win, and resist the things which by ourselves we would have been powerless to resist.

In the moment of true repentance we are liberated from the estrangement and the fear of the past, and we are equipped to face the battles of the future.

THE CHARACTERISTICS OF THE CHURCH

Acts 2 : 42-47

> They persevered in listening to the apostles' teaching, in the fellowship, in the breaking of bread and in prayers. Awe was in every soul ; and many signs and wonders were done by the apostles. All the believers were together and they were in the habit of selling their goods and possessions and of distributing them amongst all as each had need. Daily they continued with one accord in the Temple, and breaking bread from house to house they received their food with joy and in sincerity of heart ; and they kept praising God and everyone liked them. Daily the Lord added to them those who were being saved.

In this passage we have a kind of lightning summary of the characteristics of the early Church.

(i) It was *a learning Church*. The word *doctrine* in verse 42 is not passive ; it is active. The phrase means that they persisted in listening to the apostles as they taught. One of the great perils of the Church is a static religion which looks back instead of forward. Just because the riches of Christ are unsearchable and inexhaustible we should ever be going forward. The Christian must journey, not looking to the sunset, but to the sunrise. We should count it a wasted day when we do not learn something new and when we have not penetrated more deeply into the wisdom and the grace of God.

(ii) It was *a Church of fellowship*. It had what someone

has called the great quality of *togetherness*. Nelson explained one of his great victories by saying, " I had the happiness to command a band of brothers." The Church is only a real Church when it is a band of brothers.

(iii) It was *a praying Church*. These early Christians knew that they could not meet life in their own strength and that they did not need to do so. They always spoke to God before they spoke with men ; they always went in to God before they went out to the world ; they could meet the problems of life because they had first met God.

(iv) It was *a reverent Church*. In verse 43 the word which the Authorised Version correctly translates fear has the idea of awe and reverence in it. It was said of a great Greek that he moved through this world as if it were a temple. The Christian lives in reverence because he knows that the whole round earth is the temple of the living God.

(v) It was *a Church where things happened*. Signs and wonders were there (verse 43). If we expect great things from God and attempt great things for God things will happen. When faith dies achievement dies. More things would happen if we believed that God and we together can make them happen.

(vi) It was *a sharing Church* (verses 44, 45). These early Christians had an intense feeling of responsibility for each other. It was said of William Morris that he never saw a drunken man but he had a feeling of personal responsibility for him. A real Christian could not bear to have too much when others have too little.

(vii) It was *a worshipping Church* (verse 46). They never forgot to visit God's house. We must remember that " God knows nothing of solitary religion." Half the thrill of a great concert or a great athletic contest is that of being one of a great body of people. Things can happen when we come together. The Spirit of God moves upon God's worshipping people.

(viii) It was *a happy Church* (verse 46). Gladness was

there.   A gloomy Christian is a contradiction in terms.
The joy of the Christian is not necessarily a boisterous
thing ; but deep in the heart of the Christian man there
is the joy that no man taketh from us.

(ix) It was *a Church of people whom others could not
help liking*. There are two Greek words for *good*. The one
is *agathos* which simply describes a thing as good.   The
other is *kalos* which means that a thing is not only good
but looks good ; that it has a winsome attractiveness
about it.   Real Christianity is a lovely thing.   There are so
many people who are good, but in them there is a streak
of unlovely hardness.   You could never go and weep your
heart out on their shoulders.   They are what someone
has called iceberg Christians.   Struthers used to say that
what would help the Church more than anything else
would be if Christians ever and again would do a *bonnie
thing*.   In the early Church there was a winsomeness on
God's people.

A NOTABLE DEED IS DONE

Acts 3 : 1-10

> Peter and John used to go up to the Temple at the
> hour of prayer at three o'clock in the afternoon ; and a
> man who had been lame from the day of his birth was
> in the habit of being carried there.   Every day they
> used to put him at the gate of the Temple which is
> called the Beautiful Gate, so that he could beg for
> alms from the people who were going into the Temple.
> When he saw Peter and John about to go into the
> Temple he asked to be given alms.   Peter fixed his
> eyes on him with John and said, " Look at us."   He
> paid attention to them because he was expecting to
> get something from them.   Peter said to him, " Silver
> and gold I do not possess, but what I have I give
> you.   In the name of Jesus Christ of Nazareth—
> walk ! " And he took him by the right hand and lifted
> him up.   Immediately his feet and ankle bones were
> strengthened, and he leaped up and stood and walked

about ; and he went into the Temple with them, walking about and leaping and praising God. Everyone saw him walking about and praising God ; and they recognized him as the man who had sat at the Beautiful Gate of the Temple to receive alms. They were filled with amazement and astonishment at what had happened to him.

THE Jewish day began at 6 o'clock in the morning and ended at 6 o'clock in the evening. Therefore, the third hour is 9 a.m. ; the sixth hour is 12 midday ; the ninth hour is 3 p.m. For the devout Jew there were three special hours of prayer—9 a.m., 12 midday and 3 p.m. They agreed that prayer was efficacious wherever it was offered ; but they always felt that it was doubly precious when it was offered in the Temple courts. It is a very interesting thing to note that the apostles still kept up the customs and the habits in which they had been trained. It was the hour of prayer, and Peter and John were going into the Temple to observe it. A new faith had come to them, but they did not use the new faith as an excuse for a licence which broke all law. They were well aware that the new faith and the old discipline could and still must walk hand in hand.

In the East it was the custom for beggars to sit begging at the entrance to a temple or a shrine. Such a place was, and still is, considered the best of all stances because, when people are on their way to worship God, they are disposed to be generous to their fellow men. W. H. Davies, the tramp poet, tells how one of his vagrant friends told him that, whenever he came into a new town, he looked for a church spire with a cross on the top, and began to beg in that area, because there, from experience, he found people most generous. Love of man and love of God must ever go hand in hand.

This incident brings us face to face with the question of miracles in the apostolic times. There are certain definite things to be said about these miracles. (i) Such miracles *did* happen. Later on in Acts 4 : 16 we read how the

Sanhedrin knew well that they must accept the miracle because they could not deny it. The enemies of Christianity would have been the first to deny miracles if they could have done so ; but they never even try to deny them. (ii) Why then did they stop ? Certain suggestions have been made. (a) There was a time when miracles were necessary. They were, as someone has put it, the bells to call people to the Christian Church. In that age they were needed as a guarantee of the truth and the power of the Christian message in its initial attack on the world. (b) At that time two special circumstances met. First, there were living apostolic men who had had an unrepeatable personal intimacy with Jesus Christ. Second, there was abroad an atmosphere of expectancy when men's minds were ready to accept anything, and when faith was in its floodtide. These two things combined produced effects which were unique. (iii) But the real question is not, " Why have miracles stopped ? " but, " Have they stopped ? " It is the simple fact that any doctor or surgeon can now do things which in the apostolic times would have been regarded as miracles. It is the universal fact that God does not do for men what man can do for himself. So God has revealed new truth and new knowledge to men, and through that revelation they are still performing miracles. As a great doctor said, " I bandage the wounds ; but God heals them." For the Christian there are still miracles on every hand if he has eyes to see.

THE CRIME OF THE CROSS

Acts 3 : 11-16

As he clung to Peter and John everyone came running to them in the colonnade which is called Solomon's, in a state of complete astonishment. When Peter saw them he said to them, " Men of Israel, why are you surprised at this ? Or why do you keep staring at us, as if we had made him walk by our own power

or goodness ? The God of Abraham and of Isaac and of Jacob, your fathers' God, has glorified His servant Jesus, whom you handed over and disowned before Pilate, when he had given judgment for His release. You disowned the holy and the just one and you asked for a man who was a murderer to be given to you as a favour. You killed the pioneer of life but God raised Him from the dead ; and we are His witnesses. And His name, through faith in His name, has given strength to this man whom you see and know. It is the faith which is through Him, which has thus given him back his health in presence of you all."

In this passage there sound three of the great dominant notes of early Christian preaching. (i) The early preachers always stressed the basic fact that the Crucifixion was the greatest crime in human history. Whenever they speak of it there is a kind of shocked horror in their voices. Jesus was the holy one and the just, whom to see should have been to love. The Roman governor himself was well aware that the crucifixion was rank injustice. Men chose a violent criminal and drove to the Cross Him who went about doing good. The early preachers tried to stab men's minds with the realisation of the sheer crime of the Cross. It is as if they said, " Look what sin can do." (ii) The early preachers always stressed the vindication of the Resurrection. It is the simple fact that without the Resurrection the Church would never have come into being. Had Jesus not risen from the dead, He would have become a memory which would have grown ever fainter and fainter. But the Resurrection was the proof that He was literally indestructible, that He was literally Lord of life and of death, that He was literally forever. The Resurrection was the final proof that behind Him there was God, and therefore a power which nothing could stop. (iii) The early preachers always stressed the power of the Risen Lord. They never regarded themselves as the sources of power but only as channels of power. They were well aware of the limitations of what they could do. They were also well aware that there was no limitation to what the Risen Christ could do through them and with them. Therein lies the secret of the Christian life. The Christian knows that so long as he thinks of what I can do and what I can be, there can be nothing but failure and frustration and fear ; but when he thinks of " not I, but Christ in me " there can be nothing but peace and power.

THE NOTES OF PREACHING

Acts 3 : 17-26

" Now, brothers, I know that it was through ignorance that you did it, just as your rulers did. But God has thus fulfilled those things which He foretold by the mouths of all the prophets that His anointed one should suffer. Repent, then, and turn so that your sins may be wiped out, so that times of refreshing may come to you from God, and so that He may send Jesus Christ who has already been preached to you. It is necessary that heaven should receive Him until the times when all things shall be restored, times of which God spoke through the mouths of His holy prophets since the world began. Moses said, ' The Lord, your God, will raise up from your brethren a prophet like me. You must listen to him in every-thing that he will say to you ; and it will be that everyone who will not listen to that prophet will be utterly destroyed from the people.' And all the prophets who spoke from Samuel and those who succeeded him, also announced the tidings of these days. You are the sons of the prophets and of the covenant which God made with your fathers when He said, ' In your seed all the nations of the earth will be blessed.' It is to you first that God, when He raised up His Son, sent Him to bless you by making each one of you turn away from your evil deeds."

ALMOST all the notes of early Christian preaching are sounded in this short passage. (i) It begins with a note of mercy and warning combined. It was in ignorance that the Jews perpetrated the terrible deed of the crucifixion ; but that ignorance is no longer possible, and, therefore, there can be no excuse for their further rejection of Jesus Christ. This note of the terrifying responsibility of knowledge sounds all through the New Testament. " If ye were blind, ye should have no sin ; but now ye say, ' We see ' ; therefore your sin remaineth " (John 9 : 41). " If I had not come and spoken unto them they had not had sin ; but now they have no cloak for their sin " (John 15 : 22). " To him that knoweth to do good, and doeth it not, to him it is sin " (James 4 : 17). To have seen the full light of the revelation of God is the greatest of privileges, but it is also the most terrible of responsibilities. (ii) The obligation that this knowledge brings is the obligation to repent and to turn. The two words go closely together. *Repent* might simply mean to change one's mind ; and it is an easier thing to change one's mind than it is to change one's life. But this change of mind is to issue in a turning away from the old way and a faring forth upon the new. (iii) This repentance will have certain consequences. It will affect the *past*. Sins will be *wiped out*. This is a vivid word. Ancient writing was upon papyrus, and the ink used had no acid in it. It therefore did not bite into the papyrus as modern ink does ; it simply lay upon the top of it. To erase the writing a man might take a wet sponge and simply wipe it away. So God wipes out the sin of the forgiven man. It will affect the *future*. It will bring times of refreshing. Into life there will come something which will be a strength in weakness and a rest in weariness. (iv) Peter then goes on to speak of the coming again of Christ. Whatever else that doctrine means, it means that history is going somewhere ; that it moves, not haphazardly, but with the purposeful tread of things upon the way. (v) Peter insists that all that has happened has been foretold. The Jews refused to assimilate the idea of a Chosen One of God who must suffer. But Peter insists that if they search their own scriptures they will find it all there. (vi) Peter reminds them of their national privilege. In a very special sense the Jews were God's chosen people. (vii) And then, finally, he lays down the inescapable truth that that very special privilege brings a very special duty ; that the privilege is not to do what they like but to do what God likes. It is not the privilege of special honour ; it is the privilege of special service.

ARREST

Acts 4 : 1-4

> While they were speaking to the people, the priests, the superintendent of the Temple and the Sadducees came upon them. They were annoyed because they were teaching the people, and proclaiming, through Jesus, the resurrection from the dead. So they laid hands upon them, and they put them under arrest until the next day, for by this time it was evening. But many who heard the word believed ; and the number of the men was about five thousand.

THE healing of the lame man had taken place within the Temple area, at a part of the Temple which was continually thronged with people. The spotlight of publicity was inevitably focussed upon the whole incident. The Gate Beautiful itself was the gate which led from the Court of the Gentiles into the Court of the Women. The Court of the Gentiles was at once the largest and the busiest of all the Temple Courts, for into it anyone of any nation could come so long as he observed the ordinary laws of decency and decorum. It was there that the money-changers had their booths, and the sellers of sacrificial victims their stalls. Round the outer boundary of the Temple area there ran two great colonnades meeting at a right angle in the corner of the Court of the Gentiles. The one was the Royal Porch, the other Solomon's Porch. They, too, were crowded with people who had come to worship, to learn and to sightsee. Clearly the whole incident and the whole series of events, would gain the widest publicity. Into this crowded scene there came the priests, the superintendent of the Temple and the Sadducees. The man whom the Authorised Version calls the captain of the Temple was an official called the *Sagan*. He was the High Priest's right-hand man, his chief of staff, his executive officer. In particular he had the oversight of the good order of the Temple. When the crowd had gathered it was inevitable that he and his Temple police should arrive on the scene. With him there came the Sadducees. The characteristic of the Sadducees was that they were the wealthy, aristocratic class. There were not many of them, but they were rich and of great influence. The whole matter annoyed them very greatly for two reasons. First, they did not believe in the resurrection from the dead ; and it was this very truth that the apostles were proclaiming. Second, just because they were wealthy aristocrats, the Sadducean party was the collaborationist party. They tried to keep on friendly terms with the Romans in order that they might retain their own wealth and comfort and prestige and power. The last thing they wanted was any disturbance of the *status quo*. The Roman government was very tolerant ; but on public disorder it was merciless. The Sadducees immediately leapt to the conclusion that, if the apostles were allowed to go on unchecked, riots and civil disorder might follow, with disastrous consequences to their status. Therefore they proposed to nip this movement in the bud ; and that is why Peter and John were so promptly arrested. It is one of the great examples of how a party of men, in order to retain their vested interests, would not themselves listen to the truth or give anyone else a chance to hear it.

BEFORE THE SANHEDRIN

Acts 4 : 5-12

So on the next day it happened that the rulers and the elders and the scribes were assembled in Jerusalem,

together with Annas the High Priest, and Caiaphas
and John and Alexander and all those who belonged
to the priestly families. So they set them in the
midst and asked them, " By what power or by what
name have you done this ? " Then Peter, filled with
the Holy Spirit, said to them, " Rulers of the people
and elders, if to-day we are being examined about
the good deed done to the infirm man, if you are
asking us by what means he has been restored to
health, let it be known to all of you and to all the
peoples of Israel that it is by the name of Jesus Christ
of Nazareth, whom you crucified and whom God
raised from the dead—it is by this name that this
man stands before you in sound health. This is the
stone which was set at naught by you builders, which
has now become the head of the corner ; and in no
other is there salvation ; for there is no other name
under heaven, given among men, by which we must
be saved."

THE court before which Peter and John were brought
was the Sanhedrin. The Sanhedrin was the supreme
court of the Jews. Even in Roman times it had the right
of arrest. The one thing it could not do was to pass the
death sentence, except in the single case of a Gentile
who trespassed on the inner courts of the Temple. The
Sanhedrin had seventy-one members. The High Priest
was *ex officio* president. In the Sanhedrin there were
priests, and all the priests were to all intents and purposes
Sadducees. Their one desire was to preserve the *status quo*
that their own emoluments might not be lessened. There
were scribes who were the experts in the traditional law.
There were Pharisees who were fanatics for the law. There
were elders who were respected men in the community.
There remain the people who are said to be of the priestly
families ; these are the same people who are sometimes
called Chief Priests. They consisted of two classes. First,
there were ex-High Priests. In the great days the High
Priesthood had been hereditary and it had been for life ;
but in the Roman times the office of High Priest was the
subject of intrigue, bribery and corruption and High

Priests rose and fell so that between 37 B.C. and 67 A.D. there were no fewer than 28 High Priests. But even after a High Priest had been deposed he often remained the power behind the throne. Second, although the High Priesthood had ceased to be hereditary it was still the prerogative of a very few families. Of the 28 High Priests already mentioned all but 6 came from 4 priestly families. The members of these families had a special prestige, and it is they who are known as the Chief Priests. Now, when we read the speech of Peter, we must remember to whom it was spoken, and when we do remember that it becomes one of the world's great demonstrations of courage. It was spoken to an audience of the wealthiest, the most intellectual and the most powerful in the land, and yet Peter, the Galilaean fisherman, stands before them rather as their judge than as their victim. But further, this was the very court which had condemned Jesus to death. Peter knew it, and he knew that at this moment he was taking his life in his hands. There are two kinds of courage. There is the reckless courage which goes on scarce aware of the dangers it is facing. There is the far higher, cool, calculated courage which knows the peril in which it stands and which will not be daunted. It was that second courage that Peter demonstrated to men. When Achilles, the great warrior of the Greeks, was told that if he went out to battle he would surely die, he answered in the immortal sentence, " Nevertheless, I am for going on." Peter, in that moment, knew the peril in which he stood ; nevertheless, he, too, was for going on.

NO LOYALTY SAVE TO GOD

Acts 4 : 13-22

When they saw how boldly Peter and John spoke, and when they had grasped the fact that they were men with no special knowledge and no special qualifications, they were amazed ; and they recognized them for men who had been in the company of Jesus. So, as they looked at the man who was cured and who was standing with them, they could find no charge to make. They ordered them to leave the Sanhedrin, and they discussed with each other, " What are we to do with these men ? for, that, through them, a notable sign has happened, is plain to all who live in Jerusalem, and we cannot deny it. But, in order that this may not spread any further throughout the people, let us forbid them with threats to speak any more in this name to any man." So they summoned them in and ordered them absolutely to abstain from teaching in the name of Jesus. But Peter and John said to them, " You must judge whether, in the sight of God, it is right to listen to you rather than to God ; for we are unable not to speak the things that we have seen and heard." But they added still further threats and let them go because they could find no means of punishing them because of the people, for everyone glorified God at what had happened, for the man on whom the sign of healing had taken place was more than forty years old.

HERE in this passage we see very vividly both the enemy's attack and the Christian defence. In the enemy's attack there are two characteristics. First, there is *contempt*. The Authorised Version says that the Sanhedrin regarded Peter and John as unlearned and ignorant men. The word translated unlearned means that they had no kind of technical education, especially in the intricate regulations and casuistry of the law. The word that is translated ignorant means that they were laymen with no special professional qualifications. The Sanhedrin, as it were, regarded them as men without a college education and with no professional status. It is often difficult for the simple man to meet what might be called academic and professional snobbery. But on the man in whose heart is Christ, there is a real dignity which neither academic attainment nor professional status can give. Second of the attacks was *threats*. They were told what would happen if they went on with the course that they had chosen.

But man's threats are powerless to deflect the Christian because he knows that anything that man does to him is but for a moment, whereas the things of God last forever. In face of this attack Peter and John had certain defences. First, they had the defence of an *unanswerable fact*. That the man had been cured it was impossible to deny. The greatest and the most unanswerable defence and proof of Christianity is a Christian man. In the last analysis words count for little. We can only prove Christianity to others by confronting them with the undeniable evidence of a Christian character. Second, they had the defence of an utter *loyalty to God*. If it was a question of choosing between obeying man and obeying God, Peter and John were in no doubt as to what course to take. As H. G. Wells said, " The trouble with so many people is that the voice of their neighbours sounds louder in their ears than the voice of God." The real secret of Christianity lies in that great tribute that was once paid to John Knox— " He feared God so much that he never feared the face of any man." But it was the third defence which was greatest of all. It was the defence of a *personal experience of Jesus Christ*. As Peter and John said, they were quite unable to stop speaking of those things which they had personally seen and heard. Their message was no carried tale. They knew at first-hand that it was true ; and they were so sure of it that they were willing to stake their life upon it.

THE TRIUMPHANT RETURN

Acts 4 : 23-31

> When they had been released, they came to their own people and they told them all that the chief priests and elders had said to them. When they had heard the story, with one accord, they lifted up their voice to God and said, " O Sovereign Lord, Thou who hast made the heaven and the earth and the sea and all that is in them, Thou who didst say, through the Holy Spirit by the mouth of David, our father, Thy

servant, ' Why did the nations rage and the people set their thoughts on empty things ? ' The kings of the earth stood around and the rulers assembled together against the Lord and against His Anointed One. For in truth in this city they were assembled against Thy holy servant Jesus, whom Thou didst anoint—Herod and Pontius Pilate, with the Gentiles and the peoples of Israel—to do all the things which Thy hand and Thy purpose fore-ordained should be done. So now, O Lord, look upon their threats and grant to Thy servants to speak Thy word with boldness, whilst Thou dost stretch out Thy hand to heal and whilst signs and wonders happen through the name of Thy holy servant Jesus." And when they had prayed the place in which they were assembled was shaken, and they were all filled with the Holy Spirit, and kept on speaking the word with boldness.

IN this passage we have the reaction of the Christian Church in the hour of danger. It might have been thought that when Peter and John returned with their story a deep depression would have fallen on the Church, as they looked ahead to the troubles which were now bound to descend upon them. The one thing that never even struck them was to obey the Sanhedrin's command to speak no more. Into their minds at that moment there came certain great convictions and into their lives there came a tide of strength. (i) They had the conviction of the *power of God*. With them was He who was creator and sustainer of all things. Once the papal envoy threatened Martin Luther with what would follow if he persisted in his course and warned him that in the end he would be deserted by all his supporters. " Where will you be then ? " demanded the envoy. " Then as now," Luther answered, " in the hands of God." For the Christian, they that are for us are always more than they that are against us. (ii) They had the conviction of the *futility of man's rebellion*. The word which the Authorised Version translates *rage* is used of the neighing of high-fed and spirited horses. They may trample and toss their heads and neigh ; in the end they will have to accept the discipline of the reins. Men may make their defiant gestures against God ; in the end God must prevail. (iii) They set before themselves the *remembrance of Jesus*. They remembered how He was tried, how He suffered and how He triumphed ; and in that memory they found their confidence, for it is always enough for the disciple that he be as his Lord. (iv) They *prayed* for courage. They did not pretend that they could face this in their own strength ; they took it to God. In the hour of trial they turned from time and stretched out to eternity ; when their own strength failed they turned to a power that was not their own. (v) The result was the *gift of the Spirit*. The promise was fulfilled ; they were not left comfortless ; it was true that He was with them always. So they found the courage and the strength they needed to witness when their witness might well mean their death.

ALL THINGS IN COMMON

Acts 4 : 32-37

> The heart and soul of the crowd who had believed was one ; and no one used to say that any of his possessions was his own, but they had all things in common. And the apostles kept on bearing witness to the resurrection of the Lord Jesus with great power, and great grace was on them all. Nor was anyone in need amongst them, for all who were owners of lands and houses made a habit of selling them and of bringing the proceeds of what they sold and of placing them at the apostles' feet. It was distributed to each, just as a man needed.
>
> Joseph, whose surname was Barnabas, one of the apostles (the translation of the name is Son of Consolation), who was a Levite and who was a native of Cyprus, possessed a field, and he sold it and brought the price and laid it at the apostles' feet.

HERE in this new paragraph there is a sudden change which is typical of Christianity. Just immediately before this all things were moving in the most exalted atmosphere. There were great thoughts of God ; there were prayers for the Holy Spirit ; there were exultant quotations from the Old Testament. And now without warning the whole narrative suddenly changes to the most practical things. However exalted these early Christians might be, however much they had their moments on the heights, they never forgot that someone was hungry, that someone had not enough and that all must help. Prayer was supremely important ; the witness of words was supremely important, but the culmination is charity and love of the brethren. Two things are to be noted about them. (i) They had an intense sense of *responsibility for each other*. It seemed to them unthinkable that anyone of them could have too much whilst another had too little. (ii) This awoke in them *a real desire to share all they had*. We must note one thing above all—this sharing was not the result of legislation ; it was utterly spontaneous. It is not when the law compels us to share, but when the heart moves us to share, that society becomes really Christian. The charity of legislation can never be a substitute for the charity of the heart.

TROUBLE IN THE CHURCH

Acts 5 : 1-11

A man called Ananias, together with his wife Sapphira, sold a bit of ground he had, and surreptitiously kept back part of the price, and his wife knew about it. He brought some part of the price and laid it at the feet of the apostles. Peter said to him, " Ananias, why has Satan filled your heart, so that you have deceived the Holy Spirit and kept back part of the price of your ground ? While it remained yours did it not remain your own, and after it had been sold was it not entirely at your disposal ? Why did you put this business into your heart ? It is not to men you have lied but to God." As Ananias listened to these words, he collapsed and breathed his life out. Great awe came upon all who heard it. The young men rose and bound him up and carried him out and buried him.

After an interval of about three hours his wife came in, and she was not aware of what had happened. Peter said to her, " Tell me, did you sell the piece of ground for so much ? " " Yes," she said, " for so much." Peter said to her, " Why is it that you agreed to tempt the Spirit of the Lord ? Look now, the feet of those who have buried your husband are at the door, and they will carry you out." Immediately she collapsed at his feet and breathed her life out. When the young men came in they found her dead and they carried her out and buried her beside her husband. And great awe came upon the whole Church and upon all who heard these things.

THERE is no more vivid story than this in the Book of Acts. There is no need to make a miracle of it. But it does show us something of the atmosphere which prevailed in the Early Church. It is on record that once Edward the First blazed with anger at one of his courtiers and the man dropped dead in sheer fear. This story shows two things about the Early Church. It shows the expectancy and the sensitivity of men's minds in those days. And it shows the extraordinary respect in which the apostles were held. In that atmosphere when life was keyed up the word and the rebuke of Peter acted like that.

This is one of the stories which demonstrate the almost stubborn honesty of the Bible. It is a story which might well have been left out because it shows that even in the Early Church there were very imperfect Christians. But the Bible refuses to present an idealised picture of anything. Once a court painter painted the portrait of Oliver Cromwell. Cromwell was disfigured by warts upon his face. The painter, thinking to please the great man, omitted the disfiguring warts in the portrait. When Cromwell saw the picture, he said, " Take it away, and paint me warts and all." It is one of the great virtues of the Bible that it shows us its heroes and its great ages, warts and all.

There is a certain encouragement in this story, for it

shows us that even in its greatest days the Church was a mixture of good and bad. We do well to remember that if the Church were a society of perfect people there would be no Church at all.

It is very significant to see how Peter insists that sin is sin against God. We would do well to remember that very specially in certain directions. (i) Failure in diligence is sin against God. God works through men. Everything, however humble it may be, that contributes to the health, the happiness and the welfare of mankind is work done for God. Antonio Stradivari, the great maker of violins, said, " If my hand slacked, I should rob God." That is a motto for every man to take. (ii) Failure to use our talents is sin against God. God gave us such talents as we have ; they are not ours ; we hold them in stewardship for Him ; and we are responsible not to men but to God for how we use them. (iii) Failure in truth is sin against God. We only know what truth is by the action of the Spirit within our hearts; and when we slip into dishonesty and falsehood it is sin against the guidance of the Spirit in our hearts.

THE ATTRACTION OF CHRISTIANITY

Acts **5** : 12-16

> Many signs and wonders were done among the people through the hands of the apostles ; and they were all together in Solomon's colonnade. Of the others no one dared to meddle with them. But the people held them in the highest esteem ; nay more, crowds of men and women believed in the Lord and attached themselves to them. The result was that they brought the sick to the streets and laid them on beds and pallets, so that, when Peter came, even his shadow might fall on some of them ; and a crowd assembled from the cities round about Jerusalem carrying the sick and those who were troubled by unclean spirits ; and all of them were healed.

HERE is a cameo-like picture of what went on in the Early Church. It tells us certain things about that Church. (i) It tells us where the Church met. Their meeting-place was Solomon's colonnade. That was one of the two great colonnades which surrounded the Temple area. These early Christians were constant in their attendance at the House of God. Daily they kept their appointment with God. They desired ever to know God better and ever to draw upon God's strength for life and living. And where could they be nearer God than in God's House ? (ii) It tells us how the Church met. The early Christian assembled in the place, where, of all places, everyone would see them. They had no idea of hiding their Christianity. They knew what had happened to the apostles and what might well at any moment happen to them ; but they were determined to show all men whose they were and where they stood. (iii) It tells us that the Early Church was a supremely effective Church. Things happened. The days when the healing ministry of the Church was in the very forefront of its work are over, although they may well return. But the Church still exists to make bad men good ; it still exists that through it the miracles of God's grace should happen. Men will always throng to a Church wherein men's lives are changed.

This passage closes with a reference to those who were troubled by unclean spirits. The ancient people attributed all disease to the agency of unclean spirits. The Egyptians, for instance, believed that the body could be divided up into separate parts and sections and that every part could be inhabited by an evil spirit. Often they believed that these evil spirits were the spirits of wicked people who had departed this life and who were still carrying on their malignant work. We may think that we have learned to see beyond that kind of belief but it was very real to them.

ARREST AND TRIAL ONCE AGAIN

Acts 5 : 17-32

But the High Priest and his party (the local sect of the Sadducees) were filled with envy, and they laid hand on the apostles and put them under public arrest. But through the night the angel of the Lord opened the doors of the prison and led them out and said, " Go, stand in the Temple and tell the people all the words of this life." When they had heard this they came into the Temple very early and began to teach. When the High Priest and those with him arrived they summoned the Sanhedrin and all the council of the sons of Israel ; and they despatched messengers to the prison that they should be brought. When the officers arrived they did not find them in the prison. When they had returned they brought news saying, " We found the prison shut with all security, and the guards standing at the doors, but when we opened the doors we found no one inside." When the superintendent of the Temple and the chief priests heard these words they did not know what to make of them and could not understand what could have happened. But someone arrived and told them, " Look now, the men you put in prison are standing in the Temple and teaching the people." Then the superintendent of the Temple went away with his officers and fetched them, but he used no force, for they were afraid of the people in case they might be stoned. When they had fetched them they stood them amidst the Sanhedrin. The High Priest questioned them, " We laid the strongest injunctions on you not to teach in this name ; and, look now, you have filled Jerusalem with your teaching and you are aiming at bringing on us guilt for the blood of this man." Peter and the apostles answered, " It is necessary to obey God rather than men. The God of our fathers raised up Jesus whom you got into your hands and hanged on a tree. God has exalted Him as Prince and Saviour at His right hand, to give repentance to Israel and remission of sins, and we are witnesses of these things, as is the Holy Spirit, whom God gave to those who obey Him."

THE second arrest of the apostles was inevitable. The Sanhedrin had strictly ordered them to abstain from teaching in the name of Jesus and they had publicly disregarded that injunction. We must always remember that to the Sanhedrin this was a doubly serious matter. First, these apostles were heretics. But second, they were potential disturbers of the peace. Palestine was always an inflammable country ; if this were not checked it might well result in some kind of popular rising ; and that was the last thing the Priests and Sadducees wanted, because then Rome would intervene and their place and prestige would be lost.

We need not necessarily see a miracle in the release of Peter and John. The word *aggelos* has two meanings. It means an angel; but it is also the normal Greek word for a messenger. Even if the release of the apostles had been brought about by human plans and human means, the agent who effected the release would still be the *aggelos* of the Lord.

In the narrative of the events after the release we see vividly displayed the great characteristics of these early men of God. (i) They were men of courage. The command to go straight back and preach in the Temple sounds to a prudent mind, whose aim is safety first, almost incredible. To obey that command was an act of almost reckless audacity. They knew what would happen and yet they went. (ii) They were men of principle. And the one principle of their lives was that at all costs and in all circumstances obedience to God must come first. They never asked, " Is this course of action safe ? " They asked, " Is this what God wants me to do ? " And then they laid aside the calculations of safety and obeyed. They were supremely willing to venture for God. (iii) They had a clear idea of their duty and their function. They knew that they were witnesses for Christ. A witness is essentially a man who speaks from first-hand knowledge. He is a man who says, " This is true and I know it." He is a man who knows from personal experience that what he says is true ; and it is impossible to stop a man like that because it is impossible to stop the truth.

THE ACTS OF THE APOSTLES

AN UNEXPECTED ALLY

Acts 5 : 33-42

When they heard this they were torn with vexation and planned to destroy them. But a certain Pharisee called Gamaliel stood up in the Sanhedrin, a teacher of the law held in honour by all the people, and ordered that the men should be put out of the meeting for a short time. He said to them, " Men of Israel, take heed to yourselves regarding these men and think what you are going to do with them. Before these days Theudas arose, saying that he was someone. Men to the number of about four hundred attached themselves to him. He was destroyed and all who were persuaded by him were dispersed and came to nothing. After him Judas the Galilaean arose, in the days when the census was taken, and he persuaded the people to follow him. He too perished and all the people who were persuaded by him were scattered abroad. And in the present circumstances I say to you—keep off these men and let them go, because if this purpose and this affair is of men it will come to nothing ; but if it is of God you cannot stop them. So take care that you do not turn out to be men who are fighting against God." They were persuaded by him. So they called in the apostles, and, when they had threatened them, they enjoined them not to speak in the name of Jesus and sent them away. So they went out from the presence of the Sanhedrin rejoicing because they were deemed worthy to suffer dishonour for the name. Every day in the Temple and from house to house they never stopped teaching and proclaiming the good news that Jesus was God's Anointed One.

ON their second appearance before the Sanhedrin the apostles found an unexpected helper. Gamaliel was a Pharisee. Now there was this basic difference between the Sadducees and the Pharisees. As we have seen, the Sadducees were the wealthy, priestly collaborationists, who were ever seeking to preserve their own prestige and their own power. The Pharisees had no political ambitions. Their name literally means " The Separated Ones," and they had separated themselves from all ordinary life and from all ordinary men in order to devote life to the keeping of the smallest detail of the law. There were never more than about six thousand of them all told, and the austerity of their lives made them highly respected. But Gamaliel was more than respected ; he was loved. He was a kindly man with a far wider tolerance than his fellows. He was, for instance, one of the very few Pharisees who did not regard Greek culture and letters as sinful and forbidden. He was one of the very few to whom the title " Rabban " had been given. Men called him " The Beauty of the Law." And when he died it was said, " Since Rabban Gamaliel died there has been no more reverence for the Law ; and purity and abstinence died out at the same time." When the Sanhedrin seemed likely to resort to violent measures against the apostles he intervened. The Pharisees had a belief which combined fate and free-will. They believed that all things were in the hand of God and yet they believed that man was responsible for his actions. " Everything is foreseen," they said, " yet freedom of choice is given." " Everything is decreed by God," they said, " except the fear of God." So Gamaliel's point was that they must have a care in case they were exercising their free-will to go against God. He pleaded that if this matter was not of God, it would come to nothing anyway. He quoted two examples. He quoted the example of Theudas. In those days, Palestine had a quick succession of fire-brand leaders who set themselves up as the deliverers of their country and sometimes even as the Messiah. Who this Theudas was we do not know. There was a Theudas who arose some years later who led a band of people out to the Jordan with the promise that he could divide the waters and that they would walk over dryshod, and whose rising was swiftly dealt with. Theudas was a common name and no doubt this was just such another fire-brand. Judas had rebelled at the time of the census. The census was taken by the governor Quirinius in 6 A.D. The purpose of the census was to arrange taxation. Judas was a fanatic who took up the position that God was the King of Israel ; to Him alone tribute was due ; and that all other taxation was impious and to pay it was a blasphemy. He attempted to raise a revolution but failed. So Gamaliel quoted these instances and declared that if this matter was not of God it would of itself fail; but if it was, nothing could stop it, and if they tried to stop it they were opposing God. The Sanhedrin listened to him. Once again they threatened the apostles and then let them go.

They went rejoicing in their tribulations. They rejoiced in persecution for two reasons. (i) It was an opportunity to demonstrate their loyalty to Christ. In Russia in the early days of Communism the man who could show the marks of the fetters on his hands and the mark of the lash on his back was the man in honour, because he had suffered for the cause. It was Mr. Valiant-for-Truth's proud boast, " My marks and scars I carry with me." (ii) It was a real opportunity to share in the experience of Christ. Those who shared in the cross-bearing would share in the crown-wearing.

THE FIRST OFFICE-BEARERS

Acts 6 : 1-7

In those days, when the number of the disciples was growing, there arose a complaint of the Greek-speaking Jews against the Hebrew-speaking Jews, in which they alleged that their widows were being overlooked in the daily distribution. The Twelve sent for the main body of the disciples and said, " It is not fitting that we should abandon the word of God to serve tables. So, brethren, look about for seven attested men from your number, men full of the Holy Spirit and of wisdom, and we will put them in charge of this business. As for us, we will give our undivided attention to prayer and to the service of the word." This seemed a good idea to the body of the disciples. So they chose Stephen, a man full of faith and of the Holy Spirit, and Philip and Prochoros and Nicanor and Timon and Parmenos and Nicolaos, who was a Gentile from Antioch who had embraced the Jewish faith. They brought these men into the presence of the apostles ; and they prayed and laid their hands upon them. So the word of God progressed and the number of disciples in Jerusalem was very greatly increased ; and a large number of the priests accepted the faith.

As the Church grew it began to encounter all the problems of an organisation and an institution. There is no nation which has always had and which still has such a sense of responsibility for the less fortunate brethren as the Jews have. In the Synagogue there was a routine custom. There were officials who were known as receivers of alms. Two collectors went round the market and round the private houses every Friday morning and made a collection partly in money and partly in goods for the needy. Later in the day this was distributed. Those who were temporarily in need received enough to enable them to carry on ; and those who were permanently unable to support themselves received enough for fourteen meals, that is enough for two meals a day for the ensuing week. The fund from which this distribution was made was called the *Kuppah* or Basket. In addition to this there was a house-to-house collection made daily for those in pressing need. This was called the *Tamhui*, or Tray. It is clear that the Christian Church had very wisely taken over this custom. But amidst the Jews themselves there was a cleavage. The rigid, orthodox Jew hated all things Gentile. In the Christian Church there were two kinds of Jews. There were the Jerusalem and the Palestinian Jews. They spoke Aramaic, the descendant of the ancestral language, and they prided themselves that there was no foreign admixture in their lives. On the other hand there were Jews from foreign countries. They had come up for Pentecost ; they had made the great new discovery of Christ and they had remained. Many of them had been away from Palestine for generations ; they had forgotten their Hebrew and they spoke Greek. The very natural consequence was that the spiritually snobbish Aramaic-speaking Jews looked down on and despised the foreign Jews. This contempt found its way into the daily distribution of alms and there was a complaint that the widows of the Greek-speaking Jews were being—very possibly deliberately—neglected. The apostles themselves could not get themselves mixed up in a matter like this. So the Seven were chosen to straighten out and to deal with this situation.

It is extremely interesting to note that the first office-bearers to be appointed were not men whose duty it was to talk ; they were chosen for practical service. Florence Alshorn, the great missionary teacher, once said, " An ideal is not yours until it comes out of your finger-tips." The first concern of the Early Church was to put its Christianity into practical action.

A CHAMPION OF FREEDOM ARISES

Acts 6 : 8-15

> Stephen, full of grace and power, performed great wonders and signs among the people. There arose in debate with Stephen certain members of the Synagogue of the Libertines and of the Cyrenians and of the Alexandrians, and of those from Cilicia and Asia ; and they could find no answer to his wisdom and to the Spirit with whose help he spoke. So they formed a plot to introduce certain men who alleged, " We heard this man speak blasphemous words against Moses and against God." So they agitated the people and the elders and the scribes, and they came upon Stephen and seized him and brought him to the Sanhedrin. Then they introduced false witnesses who alleged, " This man never stops saying things against the holy place and against the law ; for we have heard him say that Jesus of Nazareth will destroy this place and will alter the customs which Moses handed down to us." And when all those who sat in the Sanhedrin gazed intently at him, they saw his face looking as if it were the face of an angel.

WHEN the Church appointed these seven men it did something with consequences which were far-reaching. In essence the great debate and the great struggle had begun. The Jews always looked on themselves as the chosen people; but they had interpreted that word *chosen* in the wrong way. They looked on themselves as chosen for special honour and for special privilege ; and they believed that God had no use for any other people than themselves. At their worst they declared that God had created the Gentiles to be fuel for the fires of hell. Even at their mildest they believed that some day the Gentiles would become their servants. They never dreamed that they were chosen for service to bring all men into the same relationship with God as they believed that they themselves enjoyed. Here was the thin end of the wedge. True, this is not yet a question of bringing in the Gentiles. It is Greek-speaking Jews who are involved. But not one of the seven has a Jewish name ; all the names are Greek ; and one of them, Nicolaos, was a Gentile who had accepted the Jewish faith, for that is what the word proselyte means. Now Stephen saw far further than his comrades. Clearly Stephen had a vision of a world for Christ. To the Jews two things were specially precious. First, there was the Temple ; there alone sacrifice could be offered and there alone God could be truly worshipped. Second, there was the Law which could never be changed. But Stephen saw that the Temple must pass away, that the Law was but a stage towards the gospel, that Christianity must go out to the whole wide world. He said so. He got a chance to say so because in the Synagogue service there was no one person to preach the sermon. Any distinguished stranger might be called upon to preach. None could withstand his arguments. So the Jews, when logic and argument failed, resorted to force and Stephen was arrested. Stephen's career was to be short ; but it was full of significance for he was the first to see that Christianity was not the perquisite of the Jews but God's offer to all the world.

STEPHEN'S DEFENCE

When Oliver Cromwell was outlining the education he thought necessary for his son Richard, he said, " I would have him know a little history." It was to the lesson of history that Stephen appealed. Stephen clearly believed that the best form of defence was attack. What he did was to take a bird's eye view of the panorama of the history of the Jewish people. There he saw certain truths emerging, truths which he used as condemnation of his own nation. (i) He saw that the men who played a really great part in the history of Israel were the men who heard God's command, " Get thee out," and who were not afraid to obey it. The great men were the men who were prepared to make the adventure of faith. With that adventurous spirit Stephen implicitly contrasted the spirit of the Jews of his own day, whose one desire was to keep things as they were and who regarded Jesus and His followers as dangerous innovators. (ii) He insisted that men had worshipped God long before there ever was a Temple. To the Jew the Temple was the most sacred of all places. Stephen's insistence on the fact that God does not dwell exclusively in any temple made with hands was a blow at all his people held sacred. (iii) Stephen insisted that when the Jews crucified Jesus they were only setting the coping stone on a policy they had followed all through their national history ; for all through the ages they had persecuted the prophets and had abandoned the leaders whom God had raised up. These were hard truths for men who believed themselves to be the chosen people, and it is little wonder that they were infuriated when they heard them. We must watch for these ever-recurring notes as we study Stephen's defence.

THE MAN WHO CAME OUT

Acts 7 : 1-7

The High Priest said, " Is this so ? " And Stephen said, " Men, brothers and fathers, listen to what I have to say. The God of glory appeared to Abraham our father when he was in Mesopotamia, before he lived in Charran. He said to him, ' Get out from your country and from your kindred and come here to a land which I will show you.' Then he came out from the land of the Chaldaeans and took up his residence in Charran. After the death of his father he removed from there and took up his residence in this land where you now live. God did not give him an inheritance in it, not even enough to set his foot upon. But He did promise him that He would some day give it to him for a possession and to his descendants after him, although at that time he had no child. God spoke thus—that his descendants would be sojourners in an alien land, that they would make slaves of them and treat them badly for four hundred years. As for the nations to which they will be slaves—God said— ' I will judge them, and after these years have passed, they will come out and they will serve Me in this place.' "

As we have already seen, it was Stephen's method of defence to take a panoramic view of Jewish history. It was not the mere sequence of events which was in Stephen's mind. To him every person and event symbolised something, was in fact a specimen and a sample of men's reactions to the commands of God. Stephen began with Abraham, for in the most literal way it was with him that, for the Jew, history began. In Abraham, Stephen sees three things. (i) Abraham was a man who answered the summons, " Get thee out." As the writer to the Hebrews put it, Abraham went out, not knowing whither he went (Hebrews 11 : 8). He was the man of the adventurous spirit. Lesslie Newbigin, the Scottish minister who has become a bishop in the Church of South India, tells us that when negotiations were proceeding towards that union, they were often held up by people who demanded just where such and such a step might lead. In the end someone had to say to these careful souls, " A Christian has no right to ask where he is going." For Stephen the man of God was the man who obeyed God's command even when he had no idea what the consequences might be. (ii) Abraham was the man of faith. He did not know where he was going but he believed that, under God's guidance, the best was yet to be. Even when he had no children, and when, humanly speaking, it seemed that it was impossible that he ever should have any children, he believed the promise that some day his descendants would inherit the land God had promised to them. Abraham was the man who believed that God's promises were true. (iii) Abraham was the man of hope. Even to the end of the day he never saw the promise fully fulfilled, but he never doubted that it would be so. So Stephen presents these Jews with the picture of an adventurous life, ever ready to answer the summons, " Get thee out," in contrast with their desire to cling to the past and never to change.

DOWN INTO EGYPT

Acts 7 : 8-16

" So He gave him the covenant of which circumcision was the sign. So he begat Isaac and he circumcised him on the eighth day. And Isaac begat Jacob and Jacob begat the twelve patriarchs. The patriarchs were jealous of Joseph and sold him into Egypt ; but God was with him and rescued him from all his troubles and gave him grace and wisdom before Pharaoh king of Egypt. So he made Joseph the ruler of Egypt and of his whole house. There came a famine upon the whole of Egypt and Canaan, and great affliction ; and our fathers could not find food. But Jacob heard that there was corn in Egypt, and he despatched our fathers there on their first visit. On the second visit Joseph's brothers discovered who he was, and Joseph's family became known to Pharaoh. So Joseph sent and invited Jacob his father to come together with all his relations, in all seventy-five persons. So Jacob came down to Egypt ; and he himself died there and so did our fathers. They were brought over to Sychem and they were laid in the tombs which Abraham had bought at the price of silver from the sons of Emmor in Sychem."

THE picture of Abraham is succeeded by the picture of Joseph. The key to Joseph's life is summed up in his own saying in Genesis 50 : 20. At that time his brothers were afraid that, after the death of his father Jacob, Joseph would take vengeance on them for what they had done to him. Joseph's answer was, " As for you, you thought evil against me ; but God meant it unto good." Joseph was the man for whom seeming disaster turned to triumph. Sold into Egypt as a slave, wrongfully imprisoned, forgotten by the men he had helped, the day yet came when Joseph became prime minister of Egypt. Stephen sums up the characteristics of Joseph in two words—God gave him *grace* and *wisdom*. (i) This word grace is a lovely word. At its very simplest it means beauty in the physical sense ; then it comes to mean that beauty of character which all men love. Its nearest English equivalent is *charm*. There was about Joseph that charm which is always on the really good man. It would have been extremely easy for Joseph to become a soured and embittered and disappointed man. But Joseph dealt faithfully with each duty as it emerged, and served with equal devotion as a slave in a prison or as prime minister of a country. He was pre-eminently the man who did with his might what his hand found to do. (ii) There is no word more difficult to define than the word *wisdom*. It means so much more than mere cleverness, or shrewdness, or intellectual grasp of truth. But the life of Joseph itself gives us the clue to the meaning of the word. In essence, wisdom is the ability to take the long view of things, to see things as God sees them. Once again the contrast is there. The Jews were lost in the contemplation of their own past and statically involved in the mazes of their own Law. But Joseph was the man who welcomed each new task, even if that task was a rebuff, the man who took the long view, which is God's view of life.

THE MAN WHO NEVER FORGOT HIS FELLOW-COUNTRYMEN

Acts 7 : 17-36

" When the time for the fulfilment of the promise which God had told to Abraham drew near, the people increased and multiplied in Egypt, until there arose another king in Egypt who had no knowledge of Joseph. He schemed against our race and treated our fathers badly by making them cast out their children so that they would not survive. At this point Moses was born and he was very comely in God's sight. For three months he was nurtured in his father's house. When he was put out Pharaoh's daughter took him up and she brought him up as her own son ; and Moses was educated in all the lore of the Egyptians. He was mighty in his words and in his deeds. When he was forty years of age the desire came into his heart to visit his brothers, the sons of Israel. He saw one of them being maltreated and went to his help ; and he struck the Egyptian and exacted vengeance for the man who was being ill-treated. He thought that his brothers would understand that God was going to rescue them through him but they did not understand. The next day he came upon the scene as two of them were fighting. He tried to reconcile them and to make peace between them. ' Men,' he said, ' you are brothers. Why do you injure each other ? ' But the one who was injuring his neighbour pushed him away and said, ' Who made you a ruler or a judge over us ? Do you intend to murder me in the way you murdered the Egyptian yesterday ? ' When Moses heard this he fled and he became a sojourner in the land of Midian. There he begat two sons. When forty years had passed, when he was in the desert in the neighbourhood of Mount Sinai, an angel appeared to him in a flame of fire in a bush. When Moses saw it he was astonished at the sight. When he approached to see what it was the voice of the Lord came to him, ' I am the God of your fathers, the God of Abraham and of Isaac and of Jacob.' Moses was afraid and dared not look. But God said to him, ' Take your shoes off your feet for the place on which you are standing is holy ground. In truth I have seen the evil that is being done to My people in

Egypt and I have heard their groaning. I have come down to rescue them. Come now—I will send you to Egypt.' This Moses whom they rejected saying, ' Who made you a ruler and judge over us ? '—this very man God despatched as ruler and rescuer by the hand of the angel who appeared to him in the bush. He led them out after he had performed wonders and signs in Egypt and at the Red Sea and in the wilderness for forty years.''

NEXT upon the scene there comes the figure of Moses. For the Jew, Moses was above all the man who answered God's command, '' Get thee out.'' Moses was quite literally the man who gave up a kingdom to answer God's summons to be the leader of His people. Our Bible story has little to tell us of the early days of Moses ; but the Jewish historians had much more to say. We know that Moses was found by Pharaoh's daughter when his parents had to put him out of their house, and that Pharaoh's daughter brought him up as her own son. But Josephus, the Jewish historian, has much more to say than that. According to him, Moses was so beautiful a child that, even when he was being carried down the street in his nurse's arms, people stopped to look at him. He was so brilliant a lad that he surpassed all others in the speed and the eagerness with which he learned. One day Pharaoh's daughter took him to her father and asked him to make him his successor on the throne of Egypt. Pharaoh agreed. Then, the tale goes on, Pharaoh took his own crown and jestingly placed it on the infant Moses' head, whereat the child snatched the crown off and refused to wear it and threw it on the ground. One of the Egyptian wise men who was standing by said that this was a sign that if he was not killed at once this child was destined to bring disaster on the crown of Egypt. But Pharaoh's daughter snatched Moses into her arms and persuaded her father not to heed the warning. When Moses grew up he became the greatest of Egyptian generals and led a victorious campaign in far-off Ethiopia where he married the princess of the land. In face of that

we can see what Moses gave up. He in actual fact gave
up a kingdom to lead his people out into the desert on a
great adventure for God. So once again Stephen is making
the same point. The great man is not the man, who like
the Jews is thirled to the past and jealous of his privileges ;
the truly great man is the man who is ready to answer
the summons, " Get thee out," and to leave the comfort
and the ease he might have had.

A DISOBEDIENT PEOPLE

Acts 7 : 37-53

"It was this man who said to the sons of Israel, ' God
will raise up a prophet from among your brothers,
like me.' It was this Moses who was in the gathering
of the people in the wilderness, with the angel who
spoke to him in Mount Sinai, and with your fathers.
It was he who received the living oracles to give to
you. But your fathers refused to be obedient to him.
They rejected him. In their hearts they turned back
to Egypt. They said to Aaron, ' Make us gods who
will go before us, for, as for this man Moses we do
not know what has happened to him.' So in those
days they made a calf and they sacrificed to the idol
they had made and they found their joy in the works
of their hands. And God turned and gave them over
to the worship of the host of heaven ; as it stands
written in the Book of the Prophets, ' Did you not
bring me slain victims and sacrifices for forty years
in the wilderness, O house of Israel ? But now you
have accepted the tabernacle of Moloch and the star
of the god Remphan, the images you have made in
order to worship them. I will take you away to live
in the lands beyond Babylon.' Our fathers possessed
the tent of witness in the wilderness, as He who spoke
instructed Moses to make it according to the pattern
which he had seen. Your fathers received it from one
generation to another, and brought it in with Joshua
at the time when they were gaining possession of the
lands of the nations whom God drove back from
before your fathers, right up to the time of David.
He found favour with God and he asked to be allowed

to find a dwelling place for the God of Jacob. But it was Solomon who built a house for Him. But the Most High does not dwell in houses made with hands. As the prophet says, ' Heaven is my throne, earth is a footstool for my feet.' ' What kind of house will you build for Me ? ' says the Lord, ' or where is the place where I will rest ? Has not My hand made all these things ?' Stiff-necked, uncircumcised in hearts and ears, you have always opposed the Holy Spirit. As your fathers did so, so do you. Which of the prophets did your fathers not persecute ? And they killed those who told beforehand the tidings of the coming of the Just One, whom you betrayed and whose murderers you became—you who received the Law by the disposition of angels—and who did not keep it."

Now the speech of Stephen begins to accelerate. All the time by implication it has been condemning the whole attitude of the Jews ; and now that implicit condemnation becomes explicit. In this closing section of his defence Stephen has woven together several strands of thought. (i) He insists on the continued and repeated rebellions and disobedience of the people. In the days of Moses they rebelled by making the golden calf. In the time of Amos their hearts went after Moloch and the star gods. The reference to the Book of the Prophets is to what we call the Minor Prophets. The quotation is actually from Amos 5 : 27. It is different from our Authorised Version because Stephen quotes not from the Hebrew but the Greek version of Amos. (ii) He insists that they have had the most amazing privileges. They have had the succession of the prophets ; the tabernacle of the witness, so called because the tables of the Law were laid up and kept in it ; the Law which was given by angels. These two things are to be put side by side—there was continuous rebellion and disobedience and continuous privilege. The more privileges a man has the greater his condemnation if he takes the wrong way. So Stephen is insisting that the condemnation of the Jewish nation is complete because in spite of the fact that they had every chance to know better they continuously and consistently rebelled against God. (iii) Stephen insists that they have quite wrongly limited God. The Temple which should have become their greatest blessing was in fact their greatest curse. They had come to worship the Temple instead of worshipping God. They had finished up with a Jewish God who lived in Jerusalem rather than a God of all men whose dwelling was the whole universe. (iv) Stephen charges them with consistently persecuting the prophets ; and then comes the crowning charge—he charges them with the murder of the Son of God Himself. And note, Stephen does not excuse them on the plea of ignorance as Peter did. It is not ignorance but rebellious disobedience which made them commit that crime. There is anger in Stephen's closing words, but there is sorrow too. There is the anger of a man who sees a people commit the most terrible of crimes ; but there is the sorrow of a man who sees a people who have refused the destiny that God offered them.

THE FIRST OF THE MARTYRS

Acts 7 : 54—8 : 1

As they listened to this their very hearts were torn with vexation and they gnashed their teeth at him. But he was full of the Holy Spirit and he gazed steadfastly into heaven and saw the glory of God and Jesus standing at God's right hand. So he said, " Look now, I see the heavens opened and the Son of Man standing at God's right hand." They shouted with a great shout and held their ears and launched themselves at him in a body. They flung him outside the city and began to stone him. And the witnesses placed their garments at the feet of a young man called Saul. So they stoned Stephen as he called upon God and said, " Lord Jesus, receive my spirit." Kneeling down he cried with a loud voice, " Lord, set not this sin to their charge." And when he had said this, he fell asleep. And Saul fully agreed with his death.

A SPEECH like this could only have one end ; Stephen had courted death and death came. But Stephen did not see their faces distorted with rage. His gaze had gone beyond time and he saw Jesus standing at the right hand of God. But when he said so this seemed to them only the greatest of blasphemies. The penalty for blasphemy, for speaking evil of God, was stoning to death (Deuteronomy 13 : 6ff). It is to be noted that this is no judicial trial. This was a lynching, because the Sanhedrin had no right to put anyone to death. It was a surge of blind, uncontrollable anger that killed Stephen.

The method of stoning was as follows. The criminal was taken to a height and thrown down. The witnesses had to do the actual throwing down. If the fall killed the man good and well; if not, great boulders were hurled down upon him until finally he died.

Now there are in this scene certain notable things about Stephen. (i) We see the secret of his courage. His secret was that beyond all that men could do to him he saw awaiting him the welcome of his Lord. He saw the martyr's death as the gateway to the throne of Christ. (ii) We see Stephen following his Lord's example. As Jesus prayed for the forgiveness of his executioners (Luke 23 : 34) so did Stephen. When George Wishart was to be executed the executioner hesitated. Wishart came to him and kissed him. " Lo," he said, " here is a token that I forgive thee." The whole lesson of history is that the man who follows Christ the whole way will find strength to do things which it seems humanly impossible to do. (iii) For Stephen the whole dreadful turmoil finished in a strange peace. He fell asleep. To Stephen there came the peace which comes to the man who has done the right thing even if the right thing kills him.

The first half of the first verse of chapter 8 goes with this section. Saul has entered on the scene. The man who was to become the apostle to the Gentiles is the man who thoroughly agreed with the execution of Stephen.

But as Augustine said, " The Church owes Paul to the prayer of Stephen." However hard he tried Saul could never forget the way in which Stephen had died. The blood of the martyrs even thus early had begun to be the seed of the Church.

THE CHURCH REACHES OUT

Chapter 8 is an intensely important chapter in the history of the Church. The Church began by being a purely Jewish institution. Acts 6 shows the beginning, the first murmurings, of the great debate about the acceptance of the Gentiles. Stephen had had a mind far above national delimitations. Now chapter 8 shows the Church reaching out. Persecution scattered the Church abroad and where they went they took their gospel. Into chapter 8 there comes Philip who, like Stephen, was one of the Seven and who is to be distinguished from the Philip who was one of the Twelve. First, Philip preached to the Samaritans. The Samaritans formed a natural bridge between Jew and Gentile for they were half Jew and half Gentile in their racial descent. Then there comes the incident of the Ethiopian eunuch in which the gospel takes still another step out to a still wider circle. As yet the Church did not know what she was doing. As yet she had no conception of a world mission and a world Church ; but now, when we read this chapter in the light of what was soon to happen, we see the Church unconsciously but irresistibly being moved towards her destiny and her task.

HAVOC OF THE CHURCH

Acts 8 : 1-4

> At that time a great persecution broke out against the Church in Jerusalem. They were all scattered abroad throughout the districts of Judaea and Samaria, except the apostles. Pious men carried Stephen away to bury him, and they mourned greatly over him.

As for Saul, he ravaged the Church. He went into house after house and dragged out both men and women and put them under arrest.

THE death of Stephen was the signal for an outbreak of persecution, which compelled the Christians to scatter and to seek safety in the remoter districts of the country. There are two specially interesting points in this short section. (i) The apostles stood fast. Others might flee for safety but they braved whatever perils might come. They succeeded in doing this for two reasons. (a) They were men of courage. Conrad tells that, when he was a young sailor learning to steer a sailing-ship, a gale blew up. The older man who was teaching him gave him but one piece of advice. " Keep her facing it," he said. " Always keep her facing it." The apostles were determined to face whatever perils threatened them. (b) But besides that, the apostles were good men. Christians they might be, but there was something about them that had won the respect of all. It is told that once a slanderous accusation was levelled against Plato. His answer was, " I will live in such a way that all men will know that it is a lie." The beauty and the power of the life of the apostles was such an impressive thing that even in a day of persecution men hesitated to lay their hands upon them. (ii) Saul, as the Authorised Version says, made havoc of the Church. The word used in the Greek denotes a brutal and sadistic cruelty. It is used of a wild boar ravaging a vineyard into which he had broken, and of a wild animal savaging a body. The contrast between the man who was savaging the Church in this chapter and the man who surrendered to Christ in the next is intensely dramatic.

IN SAMARIA

Acts 8 : 5-13

Those who were scattered abroad went throughout the country telling the message of the good news.

Philip went down to the city of Samaria and preached Christ to them. The crowds listened attentively to what Philip had to say, as they heard his story and saw the signs which he performed. Many of them had unclean spirits, and the spirits, shouting loudly, came out of them ; and many who were paralysed and lame were cured ; and there was much rejoicing in that city.

A man called Simon was in the habit of practising magic in the city and of bewildering the people of Samaria. He alleged that he was someone great. Everyone, small and great alike, was greatly impressed by him for they said, " This man is the power of God called great." They were impressed by him because they had been bewildered by his magical deeds for some considerable time. Both men and women were baptized when they believed Philip as he told them the good news of the Kingdom of God and of the name of Jesus Christ. Even Simon himself believed, and, after he had been baptized, he was constantly in Philip's company ; and he was amazed when he saw the signs and great deeds of power which were happening.

WHEN the Christians were scattered abroad, Philip, who had emerged into prominence as one of the Seven, arrived in Samaria ; and there he preached. Now this whole incident of the work in Samaria is an astonishing thing because it was proverbial that the Jews had no dealings with the Samaritans (John 4 : 9). The quarrel between the Jews and the Samaritans was centuries old. Away back in the eighth century B.C. the Assyrians had conquered the Northern Kingdom whose capital was Samaria. As conquerors did in those days, they had transported the greater part of the population and had settled strangers in the land. In the sixth century the Babylonians conquered the Southern Kingdom with its capital at Jerusalem and its inhabitants were carried away to Babylon; but they completely refused to lose their identity and remained stubbornly Jews. In the fifth century B.C. they were allowed to return and to rebuild their shattered city and Ezra under Nehemiah. In the meantime, those of the Northern Kingdom who had been left in Palestine had intermarried with the stranger races who had been brought in. By so doing they had lost their racial purity and that for a Jew was an unforgivable crime. When the people of the Southern Kingdom returned and set to to build their city, the people round Samaria, who had never been away and who had intermarried, offered their help. It was contemptuously refused because they were not pure Jews. And from that day onwards there was an unhealed breach and a bitter hatred between Jews and Samaritans. The fact that Philip preached there, that the apostles came there, that the message of Jesus was given to these people, shows the Church all unconsciously taking one of the most important steps in history. Without realising it they are discovering that Christ is for all the world. We know very little about Philip but he was one of the architects of the Christian Church.

We must note what Christianity brought to these people (i) It brought the story of Jesus. It brought quite simply the message of the love of God in Jesus Christ. (ii) It brought healing. Christianity has never been a thing of words only. It brought light to men's minds and healing to their bodies. (iii) It brought, as a very natural consequence of this, a joy that these Samaritans had never known before. It is a counterfeit Christianity which brings an atmosphere of gloom ; the real thing radiates joy wherever it comes.

THINGS WHICH CANNOT BE BOUGHT AND SOLD

Acts 8 : 14-25

> When the apostles in Jerusalem heard that Samaria had received the word of God, they despatched Peter and John to them. They came down and prayed for them, so that they might receive the Holy Spirit, for as yet the Holy Spirit had fallen on no one. It was in the name of the Lord Jesus that they had

been baptized. Then they laid their hands on them and they received the Holy Spirit. When Simon saw that the Holy Spirit was given through the laying on of the apostles' hands, he brought money to them and said, " Give me too this power so that he on whom I lay my hands may receive the Holy Spirit." Peter said to him, " May your silver perish with you because you thought to obtain the gift of God for money ; you have neither part nor lot in this matter, for your heart is not right before God. Repent of this wickedness of yours and pray God if it may be that the intention of your heart may be forgiven you. For I see that you are in the gall of bitterness and in the bond of wickedness." Simon answered, " Do you pray to the Lord for me, so that none of the things you spoke of may come upon me."

So after they had borne their witness and spoken the word of God, they returned to Jerusalem and they told the good news to many villages of the Samaritans.

SIMON was by no means an unusual type of character in the ancient world. There were many astrologers and soothsayers and magicians, and in a credulous age they had a great influence and made a very comfortable living. There is little to be surprised at in that when even the twentieth century has not risen above fortune-telling and astrology, as almost any popular newspaper or magazine can witness. It is not by any means to be thought that Simon and his fellow-practitioners were all conscious frauds and impostors. Many of them had deluded themselves before they deluded others. They believed in their own powers.

To understand just what Simon was getting at we have to understand something of the atmosphere and practice of the Early Church. In the Early Church the coming of the Spirit upon a man was connected with certain quite definite and visible phenomena. In particular it was connected with the gift of speaking with tongues (cp. Acts 10 : 44-46). When the Holy Spirit did come upon a man he experienced an ecstasy which manifested itself in this strange phenomenon of uttering meaningless sounds. It may sound strange but for all that it was very impressive. In Jewish practice the laying on of hands was very common. When hands were laid on there was held to be a transference of certain qualities from one person to another. We still use the custom at the ordination of ministers. It is not for a moment to be thought that this represents an entirely materialistic view of the transference of the Spirit. The dominating factor was the character of the man who laid on the hands. The apostles were men who were held in such respect and admiration and even veneration that simply to feel the touch of their hands was a deeply spiritual experience. If a personal reminiscence may be allowed, I myself remember being taken to see a man who had been one of the Church's great scholars and saints. I was very young and he was very old. I was left with him for a moment or two and in that time he laid his hands upon my head and blessed me. And to this day, more than thirty years afterwards, I can still feel the thrill of that moment. In the Early Church the laying on of hands was like that.

Simon was impressed with the visible effects of the laying on of hands and he tried to buy the ability to do what the apostles could do. Simon has left his name on the language for the word *simony* still means the unworthy buying and selling of ecclesiastical offices. Simon had two faults. (i) He was not really interested in bringing the Holy Spirit to others ; he was interested in the power and the prestige it would bring to himself. This exaltation of self is ever the danger of the preacher and the teacher. It is true that the preacher and the teacher must kindle at the sight of men ; but it is also true—as Denney said—that we cannot at one and the same time show that we are clever and that Christ is wonderful. (ii) Simon forgot that there are certain gifts which are dependent on character. Money cannot buy them. Again, the preacher and the teacher must take warning. " Preaching is truth through personality." To bring the Spirit to others a man must not be a man of wealth but a man who himself possesses the Spirit.

CHRIST COMES TO AN ETHIOPIAN

Acts 8 : 26-40

The angel of the Lord spoke to Philip and said, " Rise and go to the south by the road that goes down from Jerusalem to Gaza ; that is Gaza that is Gaza in the desert." So he arose and went. Now, look you, an Ethiopian eunuch, an influential official of Candace the queen of the Ethiopians, who was in charge of all her treasury and who had gone to worship in Jerusalem, was on his way home. As he sat in his chariot he was reading the prophet Isaiah. The Spirit said to Philip, " Go and join yourself to this chariot." So Philip ran up and heard him reading the prophet Isaiah and said, " Do you understand what you are reading ? " He said, " How could I do that unless someone were to guide me ? " He invited Philip to get up and to sit with him. The passage of Scripture which he was reading was this—He was led as a sheep to the slaughter, and as a lamb before his shearer is dumb, so he did not open his mouth. In his humiliation he received no justice. Who will recount his lineage because his life is taken from the earth ? The eunuch said to Philip, " Tell me, please, who is the prophet speaking about ? Is it about himself ? Or about someone else ? " Philip opened his mouth, and, taking his start from this passage of Scripture, told him the good news about Jesus. As they were going along the road they came to some water. " Look," said the eunuch, " here is water. What is to stop me being baptized ? " And he ordered the chariot to stand still. So both Philip and the eunuch went down into the water, and he baptized him. When they came up out of the water the Spirit of the Lord carried Philip away and the eunuch no longer saw him, for he travelled along his road rejoicing. But Philip was found at Azotus. He went through all the cities and preached the good news to them until he came to Caesarea.

THERE was a road from Jerusalem which led via Bethlehem and Hebron and which joined the main road to Egypt just south of Gaza. There were two Gazas. Gaza had been destroyed in war in 93 B.C. and a new Gaza had been built to the south in 57 B.C. The first Gaza was called Old or Desert Gaza to distinguish it from the other. This road which led by Gaza would be a road where the traffic of half the world went by ; it was a road where Philip would be entirely likely to meet some adventure for Christ. Along the road in his chariot there came the Ethiopian eunuch. He was the chancellor of the exchequer of Candace. Candace is not so much a proper name as a title, the title which all the queens of Ethiopia bore. This eunuch had been to Jerusalem to worship. He must have been one of two things. In those days the world was full of people who were weary of the many gods and the loose morals of the nations. They came to Judaism and there they found the one God and the austere moral standards which gave life meaning. If they accepted Judaism and were circumcised and took the Law upon themselves they were called *proselytes* ; if they did not go that length but continued to attend the Jewish synagogues and to read the Jewish scriptures they were called *God-fearers*. So this Ethiopian must have been one of these searchers who came to rest in Judaism either as a proselyte or a God-fearer. He was reading the 53rd chapter of Isaiah ; and beginning from it Philip showed him who Jesus was.

When he became a believer he was baptized. It was by baptism and circumcision that the Gentile entered the Jewish faith. In New Testament times baptism was largely adult baptism, not that there was anything against infant baptism, but in those early days men and women were coming in from other faiths and the Christian family had hardly had time to develop. To these early Christians baptism was, whenever possible, by immersion and in running water. It symbolized three things. (i) It symbolized cleansing. As a man's body was cleansed by the water, so his soul was bathed in the grace of Christ. (ii) It marked a clean break in life. We are told how one missionary when he baptized his converts made them enter the river by one bank, baptized them, and sent them out on the other bank, as if at the moment of baptism a line had been drawn in their lives which sent them out to a new world. (iii) Baptism was a real union with Christ. As the waters closed over a man's head he seemed to die with Christ and as he emerged he rose with Christ, a new man to a new life (cp. Romans 6 : 1-4).

Tradition has it that this eunuch went home and evangelized Ethiopia. We can at least be sure that he who went on his way rejoicing would not be able to keep his newfound joy to himself.

SURRENDER

Acts 9 : 1-9

> But Saul, still breathing out threat and murder to the disciples of the Lord, went to the High Priest and asked him for letters of credit to Damascus, to the Synagogues there, so that if he found any of The Way there, both men and women, he might bring them bound to Jerusalem. As he journeyed he came near Damascus. Suddenly a light from heaven flashed round about him. He fell on the ground and he heard a voice saying to him, " Saul, Saul, why do you persecute Me ? " He said, " Who, are you, Sir ? " He said, " I am Jesus whom you are persecuting. But rise ; go into the city, and you will be told what to do." His fellow-travellers stood speechless in amazement, because they heard the voice but saw no one. So Saul rose from the ground but when his eyes were opened he could see nothing. So they took him by the hand and led him into Damascus. And for three days he could not see, nor did he eat or drink anything.

IN this passage we have the most famous conversion story in all history. We must try as far as we can to enter into Paul's mind. When we do, we will see that this is not a sudden conversion ; but it is a sudden surrender. Something about Stephen lingered in Paul's mind and would not be banished. How could a bad man die like that? In order to still this insistent doubt Paul plunged into the most violent action possible. It often happens that, when a man sets out on some action of the rightness of which he has certain doubts, he redoubles his efforts and drives himself all the harder to convince himself that he is right and to silence the doubts. His first action was to persecute the Christians in Jerusalem. This only made matters worse because once again he was bound to ask himself what secret these simple people had which made them face peril and suffering and loss absolutely serene and unafraid. So then, still plunging into ever more violent action and still driving himself on, he went to the Sanhedrin. The writ of the Sanhedrin ran wherever there were Jews. Paul had heard that certain of the Christians had escaped to Damascus and he asked for letters of credit that he might go to Damascus and extradite them. The journey only made matters worse. It was about 140 miles from Jerusalem to Damascus. The journey would be made on foot and would take about a week. Paul's only companions were the officers of the Sanhedrin, a kind of police force. Because he was a Pharisee, he could have nothing to do with them; so he walked alone; and as he walked he thought, because there was nothing else to do. The way went through Galilee, and Galilee brought this Jesus even more vividly to Paul's mind. The tension in his inner being tightened. So he came near Damascus. Damascus was one of the oldest cities in the world. Just before Damascus the road climbed Mount Hermon, and down below lay Damascus, a lovely white city in a green plain, " a handful of pearls in a goblet of emerald " as someone had called her. That very region had one characteristic phenomenon. When the hot air of the plain met the cold air of the mountain range, violent electrical storms resulted. Just at that moment there came such a lightning storm, and out of the storm Christ spoke to Paul. And in that moment the long battle was over and Paul surrendered to Christ.

So into Damascus he went a changed man. And what a change was there ! He who had intended to enter Damascus like an avenging fury was led by the hand into that city, blind and helpless as a child.

There is all of Christianity in the thing that the Risen Christ said to Paul. Christ said to him, " Go into the city, and you will be told what to do." Up to this moment Paul had been doing what *he* liked, what *he* thought best, what *his* will dictated. From this time forward he would be told what to do. Never again would he take his way, but ever after Christ's way. The Christian is a man who has ceased to do what he wants to do and who has begun to do what Jesus Christ wants him to do.

A CHRISTIAN WELCOME

Acts 9 : 10-18

There was a disciple in Damascus called Ananias, and the Lord said to him in a vision, " Ananias." He said, " Here am I Lord." The Lord said to him, " Get up and go to the street called ' Straight ' ; inquire in Judas' house for a man called Saul, a man from Tarsus. For, look you, he is praying ; and he has seen a man called Ananias coming and putting his hands on him so that he may get back his sight." Ananias answered, " Lord, I have heard from many about this man. They have told me all the hurt he has done to the saints at Jerusalem. They have told me too how he has authority from the chief priests to bind all who call upon your name." The Lord said to him, " Go, for he is a chosen instrument for My work. He is chosen to carry My name before peoples and kings and before the sons of Israel. I will tell him all he must suffer for My name's sake." So Ananias went away and came to the house. He put his hands on him and said, " Brother Saul, the Lord— Jesus who appeared to you in the way on which you were going—has sent me that you may get your sight back and so that you may be filled with the Holy Spirit." Thereupon things like scales fell from his eyes and he got his sight back again. He rose and was baptized ; and he took food and his strength increased.

BEYOND a doubt Ananias is one of the forgotten heroes of the Christian Church. If it be true that the Church owes Paul to the prayer of Stephen, it is also true that the Church owes Paul to the brotherliness of Ananias. Paul's reputation had gone before him. To Ananias there came the message from God that he must go and help Paul. He is directed to the street that is called " Straight." This was a great street that ran straight from the east to the west of Damascus. It was divided into three parts, a centre part where the traffic ran, and two side-walks where the pedestrians thronged and where the merchant-men, under canvas awnings, sat in their little booths and plied their trade. When that message came to Ananias it must have sounded mad to him. God said to Ananias, " Go and help the man who came here to throw you into prison and who would have liked to murder you." He might so well have approached Paul with suspicion, as one who was doing an unpleasant task ; he might so well have begun with recriminations and blame ; but no ; his first words are, " *Brother Saul.*" What a welcome was there ! It is one of the sublimest examples of Christian love and Christian forgiveness. That is what Christ can do. Bryan Green tells that after one of his campaigns in America he asked at the last meeting that people should stand up and in a few words say just what this campaign had done for them. A negro girl rose. She was not a good speaker ; she could only put a few sentences together and this is what she said, " Through this campaign I have found Christ and He made me able to forgive the man who murdered my father." He made me able to forgive ... that is the very essence of Christianity. In Christ, Paul and Ananias, the men who had been the bitterest enemies, came together as brothers.

WITNESSING FOR CHRIST

Acts 9 : 19-22

> Paul remained with the disciples in Damascus for
> some time. And immediately he began to preach
> Jesus in the Synagogues, and the burden of his preach-
> ing was, " This is the Son of God." Everyone who
> heard him was astonished and kept saying, " Is not
> this the man who at Jerusalem sacked those who
> call on this name? He came here too to bring them
> bound to the chief priests." But Saul's power grew
> ever greater, and he confounded the Jews who lived
> in Damascus, by proving that this is God's Anointed
> One.

THIS is Luke's account of what happened to Paul after his
conversion. If we want to have the chronology of the whole
period in our minds we must also read Paul's own account
of the matter which we have in Galatians 1 : 15-24. When
we put the two accounts together we find that the whole
chain of events runs like this. (i) Saul is converted on the
Damascus Road. (ii) He preaches in Damascus. (iii) He
goes away to Arabia (Galatians 1 : 17). (iv) He returns
and preaches in Damascus for a period of three years
(Galatians 1 : 18). (v) He goes up to Jerusalem. (vi) He
escapes from Jerusalem to Caesarea. (vii) He returns
to the regions of Syria and Cilicia (Galatians 1 : 21).
So then, when we put Luke's narrative and Paul's own
account together we see that Paul began by doing two
things. (i) He immediately bore his witness in Damascus,
in the Synagogues. In Damascus there were many Jews.
In such a town there would be far more than one Synagogue,
for in the ancient world Synagogues were as plentiful as
Churches are to-day. It was in these Damascus Synagogues
that Paul first lifted up his voice for Christ. That was an
act of the greatest moral courage. It was to these very
Synagogues that Paul had received his letters of credit as
an official agent of the Jewish faith and of the Sanhedrin.
It would have been very much easier to begin his Christian
witness somewhere where he was not known and where

his past did not stand against him. Paul at this time is saying, " I am a changed man and I am determined that those who know me best should know it." Already he is proudly saying, " I am not ashamed of the gospel of Christ." (ii) The second thing he did is not mentioned by Luke at all. Paul tells us in Galatians I : I7, " I went away into Arabia." Into Paul's life there had come this shattering change and just for a little time he had to be alone with God. Before him there stretched a new and different life. Therefore first of all Paul sought God. He needed two things. He needed guidance for a way that was totally strange to him ; and he needed strength for an almost overwhelming task that had been given to him. And he went to God for both. He had had his vision from God and now he sought from God the power to carry it out.

ESCAPING BY THE SKIN OF HIS TEETH

Acts 9 : 23-25

> After some time the Jews formed a plot to murder him ; but Saul was informed of their plot. Night and day they kept continuous watch on the gates to murder him. But the disciples took him by night, and, by way of the wall, let him down in a basket.

THIS is a vivid example of how much a single sentence in the biblical narrative may imply. Luke says that *after some time* in Damascus these things happened. The period which is dismissed in that passing phrase was a period of no less than three years (Galatians I : I8). So for three years Paul worked and preached in Damascus. The Jews were so determined to kill him that they even set a guard on the gates lest he should slip away and escape them. But the ancient cities were walled cities and the walls were often wide enough for a chariot to be driven round the top of them. On these walls there were houses whose windows often projected over the walls. In the dead of night Paul was taken into one of these houses and let down with ropes in a basket and so he was smuggled out of Damascus and was on his way to Jerusalem. So Paul's adventurous career has begun. He is only at the gateway of his adventures for Christ but even there he is escaping by the skin of his teeth and he has taken his life in his hands.

The whole incident is a witness to two things about Paul. (i) It is a witness to his courage. He must have seen the threat gathering against him in the Synagogues. He knew what had happened to Stephen and he knew what could happen to him. He knew what he had intended to do to the Christians and he knew that that very thing was liable to happen to him. Clearly Christianity for him was not going to be easy but the whole tone of the incident, for him who can read between the lines, shows that Paul revelled in these dangers. They gave him a chance to show his new-found loyalty to that Master whom he had persecuted and who had become that Master whom he loved, and would gladly have died, to serve. (ii) It is a witness to the effectiveness of Paul's preaching and witness. He was so unanswerable that when the Jews were helpless in debate they resorted to violence. No one persecutes a man who is ineffective and who obviously does not matter. George Bernard Shaw once said that the biggest compliment you can pay an author is to burn his books. Someone has said, " A wolf will never attack a painted sheep." Counterfeit Christianity is always safe. Real Christianity is always in peril. To suffer persecution is to be paid the greatest of compliments because it is the certain proof that men think we really matter.

REJECTED IN JERUSALEM

Acts 9 : 26-31

When he arrived in Jerusalem he tried to make contact with the disciples. They were all afraid of him because they did not believe that he was a disciple. But Barnabas took him and brought him to the apostles and told them the story of how, upon the road, he had seen the Lord, and that he had spoken with Him, and that in Damascus he had spoken boldly in the name of Jesus. He went in and out with them in Jerusalem, speaking boldly in the name of the Lord. He talked and debated with the Greek-speaking Jews but they tried to murder him. When the brethren got news of this they took him down to Caesarea and sent him off to Tarsus.

So the Church all over Judaea and Galilee and Samaria enjoyed peace as it was being built up ; and, walking in the fear of the Lord and in the comfort of the Holy Spirit, it was constantly increased.

WHEN Paul arrived in Jerusalem he found himself regarded with the gravest suspicion and distrust. How could it be otherwise ? It was in that very city that he had made havoc of the Church and had dragged men and women to prison. We have seen how at crucial moments in his career certain people were instrumental in winning Paul for the Church. First, the Church owed Paul to the prayer of Stephen. Then the Church owed Paul to the forgiving spirit of Ananias. And now we see that the Church owed Paul to the large-hearted charity of Barnabas. When everyone else was steering clear of Paul and suspecting him of the worst, Barnabas took him by the hand and stood sponsor for him. By this action Barnabas showed himself to be a really Christian man. (i) He was a man who insisted on believing the best of others. When others suspected Paul of merely being a spy and an *agent provocateur* Barnabas insisted on believing that he was genuine and real. The world is largely divided into people who think the best of others and people who think the worst of others ; and it is one of the curious facts of life that ordinarily we see our own reflection in others, and we make them what we believe them to be. If we insist on regarding a man with suspicion, we will end by making him do suspicious things. If we insist on believing in a man, we will end by compelling him to justify that belief. As Paul himself said, " Love thinks no evil." No one believed in men as Jesus Himself did and it is enough for the disciple that he be as his Lord. (ii) He was a man who never held a man's past against him. It is so often the case that just because a man once made a mistake, he is in our eyes forever condemned. It is the great characteristic of the heart of God that He has not held our past sins against us. We too should never condemn a man because once he failed.

Here in this passage we see Paul taking characteristic action. He disputed with the Greek-speaking Jews. Now Stephen had been one of these Hellenists. And in all probability Paul went to these very Synagogues, where once he had opposed Stephen, to witness to the fact that his life was changed. Paul was always a man who was prepared to look his past in the face, which is the hardest thing in life to do.

And here again we see Paul in peril of his life. For Paul, life had become a thing of hairbreadth escapes. Out of Jerusalem Paul was smuggled to Caesarea and thence to Tarsus. Once again he is following the consistent policy of his life, for he goes back to his native city to tell them there that he is a changed man and that the one who changed him is Jesus Christ.

THE ACTS OF PETER

Acts 9 : 32-43

> In the course of a tour of the whole area, Peter came down to the saints who lived at Lydda. There he found a man called Aeneas who had been bed-ridden for eight years. He was paralysed. So Peter said to him, " Aeneas, Jesus Christ heals you. Rise and make your bed." At once he stood up and all who lived at Lydda and at Sharon saw him, and they turned to the Lord.

In Joppa there was a disciple called Tabitha—Dorcas is the translation of her name. She was full of good works, and of deeds of charity she never stopped doing. It happened that at that time she fell ill and died. They bathed her body and placed her in an upper room. Now Lydda is near Joppa and the disciples heard that Peter was there. So they sent two men to him to invite him, " Do not fail to come to us." Peter rose and went with them. When he had arrived they took him to the upper room. And all the widows stood by in tears, showing him the coats and tunics that Dorcas used to make when she was with them. Peter put them all out and knelt down and prayed. He turned to her body and said, " Tabitha, rise." She opened her eyes and she saw Peter and sat up. He gave her his hand and raised her to her feet. He called the saints and the widows and set her before them alive. This event became known throughout the whole of Joppa and many believed on the Lord ; and Peter remained some time in Joppa, staying with a man Simon, a tanner.

FOR a time Paul has held the centre of the stage ; but now once again Peter commands the limelight. This passage really follows on from 8 : 25. It shows us Peter in action. But it shows us more than that. In the most definite way it shows us the source of Peter's power. When Peter healed Aeneas, he did not say, " I heal you " ; he said, " Jesus Christ heals you." Before he spoke to Tabitha—the name Tabitha is the Hebrew for a *gazelle* and Dorcas is the Greek for the same word—Peter prayed. It was not his own power on which Peter called ; it was the power of Jesus Christ his Lord. Peter would never have claimed to be a source of power ; he was only a channel of power. We think too much of what we can do and too little of what Christ can do through us.

There is one very interesting word in this passage. Twice the Christians at Lydda are called *saints* (verses 32 and 41). The same word is used earlier in the chapter by Ananias to describe the Christians at Jerusalem (verse 13). This is the word that Paul always uses to describe the Church member, for he always writes his letters to the saints that are at such and such a place. The word used is a Greek word *hagios*. It is a word with far-reaching associations. It is sometimes translated *holy*. But the root meaning of it is *different*. It describes something which is different from the ordinary run of things. Therefore, basically, the Christian is a man who is *different* from the people who are merely people of the world. But wherein does that difference lie ? This word *hagios* was specially used of the people Israel. They are specifically a *holy* people, a *different* people. Their difference lay in the fact that of all nations God had chosen them to be His people and to do His work. Now Israel failed in her destiny. She was disobedient and she rebelled against God. By her actions she lost her privileges and the *Church* became the true Israel. The Church became the people of God who were different. That is why this word is used to describe the Church member. Once Israel had been uniquely the *different* people ; now the Christians are the true Israel and the people who are *different*. And their difference lies in the fact that they are chosen for the special purposes of God. So then we are not different from others in that we are chosen for greater honour, greater prestige, greater glory on this earth ; we are different in that we are chosen for a greater task and for a greater service. We are saved to serve.

A DEVOUT SOLDIER

Acts 10 : 1-8

There was a man in Caesarea called Cornelius. He was a centurion in the battalion called the Italian battalion. He was a devout man and a God-fearer with all his household. He did many an act of charity to the people and he was constant in prayer to God. About three o'clock in the afternoon in a vision he clearly saw the angel of God coming to him and saying, " Cornelius." He gazed at him and he was awe-stricken. He said, " What is it, sir ? " He said to him,

" Your prayers and your works of mercy have gone up to God for a memorial ; so now, send men to Joppa, and send for a man called Simon who is also called Peter. He is lodging with one Simon a tanner, whose house is on the sea-shore." When the angel who was speaking to him went away, he called two of his servants and a devout soldier who was one of his orderlies. He told them everything and despatched them to Joppa.

THE tenth chapter of Acts tells a story that is one of the great turning points in the history of the Church. For the first time a Gentile is to be admitted into the fellowship of the Christian Church. Since Cornelius is so important a person in the history of the Church let us gather together what we can learn about him. (i) Cornelius was a Roman Centurion stationed at Caesarea, where the headquarters of the government of Palestine were. The word which the Authorised Version translates *band* and which we have translated *battalion* is the Greek word for a cohort. In the Roman military set-up there was first of all the *legion.* It was a force of six thousand men and therefore was roughly equal to a division. In every legion there were ten *cohorts.* A cohort therefore had six hundred men in it and comes near to being the equivalent of a battalion. The cohort was divided into *centuries* and over each century there was a *centurion.* The century is therefore roughly the equivalent of a company. The parallel to the centurion in our military organisation is a company sergeant-major. These centurions were the backbone of the Roman army. An ancient historian describes the qualifications of the centurion like this, " Centurions are desired not to be over-bold and reckless so much as good leaders, of steady and prudent mind, not prone to take the offensive to start fighting wantonly, but able when overwhelmed and hard-pressed to stand fast and die at their posts." Cornelius therefore was a man who first and foremost knew what courage and loyalty were. (ii) Cornelius was a *God-fearer.* In New Testament times this had become almost a technical term for Gentiles who, weary of the many gods and the immoralities and the frustration of their ancestral faiths, had attached themselves to the Jewish religion. They did not accept circumcision and the Law ; but they attended the Synagogue and they believed in one God and in the pure ethic of Jewish religion. Second then, Cornelius was a man who was seeking after God, and as he sought God, God found him. (iii) Cornelius was a man given to charity. He was a man who was characteristically a kind man. His search for God had made him love men, and he who loves his fellow men is not far from the Kingdom. (iv) He was a man of prayer. Perhaps as yet he did not clearly know the God to whom he prayed ; but, according to the light that he had, Cornelius lived close to God.

PETER LEARNS A LESSON

Acts 10 : 9-16

On the next day, when they were on the way and when they were getting near the city, about midday Peter went up to the housetop to pray. He became hungry and he wanted something to eat. When they were preparing the meal a trance came upon him. He saw the heavens opened and he saw a kind of vessel coming down. It was like a great sheet and it was let down by the four corners to the earth. On it there were all four-footed animals, all animals that creep on the earth, and all that fly in the air. A voice came to him, " Rise, Peter, kill and eat." But Peter said, " By no means, Lord, because I have never eaten anything common or unclean." And the voice spoke again the second time, " What God has cleansed, do not you reckon common or unclean." This happened three times ; and thereupon the sheet was taken up into heaven.

BEFORE Cornelius could be welcomed into the Church, Peter had to learn a lesson. The strict Jew believed that God had no use for the Gentiles, that God's favour extended to the Jews and to the Jews alone. Sometimes they even went the length of saying that help must not be given to a

Gentile woman in the time of childbirth, because that would only be to bring another Gentile into the world. Peter had to unlearn that before Cornelius could get in. There is one point which shows that Peter was on the way to unlearning some of the rigidness in which he had been brought up. He was staying with a man called Simon who was a tanner (9 : 43; 10 : 5). The trade of a tanner was unclean. He worked with the dead bodies of animals and therefore he was permanently unclean (Numbers 19 : 11-13). No rigid Jew would have dreamed of accepting hospitality from a tanner. It was his uncleanness that made it necessary for Simon to dwell on the sea-shore outside the city. But there was Peter staying with such a man. No doubt this tanner was a Christian and Peter had begun to see that Christianity abolished these petty laws and tabus. At midday Peter went to the roof to pray. In those days the house-roofs were flat ; since the houses were small and crowded people often went up to the roof for privacy and quiet. There he saw the great sheet let down. Perhaps above the flat roof there stretched an awning to ward off the heat of the sun. And maybe the awning became in Peter's trance the great sheet. The word for *sheet* is the same word as for a ship's *sail*. Maybe on the roof Peter was looking out on the blue waters of the Mediterranean and saw the ships' sails in the distance and they wove themselves into his vision. In any event the sheet with the animals on it appeared to him and the voice told him to kill and eat. Now the Jews had strict food laws. These laws are in Leviticus 11. Generally speaking the Jew might only eat animals which chewed the cud and whose hoofs were cloven. All others were *unclean* and forbidden. Peter was shocked and protested that he had never eaten anything that was unclean. The voice told him not to call what God had cleansed common or unclean. This happened three times so that there could be no possible mistake or dodging of the lesson. Once Peter would have called a Gentile unclean ; but now God is preparing him for the visitors who would come. In the trance of moments Peter has to unlearn the habits and the traditions of a lifetime.

THE MEETING OF PETER AND CORNELIUS

Acts 10 : 17-33

When Peter was at a loss in his own mind to know what this vision could mean, look you, the men who had been sent by Cornelius had asked their way to Simon's house and stood at the door. They spoke and asked if Simon who was also called Peter was lodging there. When Peter was still thinking about the vision the Spirit said to him, " Look you, three men are looking for you. Rise and go down and go with them without any hesitation, because it is I who sent them." So Peter came down to the men and said, " Look you, I am the man you are looking for. Why have you come ? " They said, " Cornelius, the centurion, a good man and a God-fearer, one to whose worth the whole nation of the Jews bears witness, was instructed by a holy angel to send for you to come to his house and to listen to the words you would give him." So he asked them in and gave them hospitality.

On the next day he rose and went with them and some of the brethren from Joppa came with him. On the next day they came to Caesarea. Cornelius was expecting them and had invited along his kinsmen and his closest friends. When Peter was going to come in Cornelius met him and fell at his feet and worshipped him. Peter raised him up and said, " Rise ; I too am a man." So he went in, talking with him as he went. He found many who had assembled there and he said, " You know that it is against the law for a man who is a Jew to have contact with or to visit one of another race. But God has shown me not to call any man common or unclean. So I came without any objection when you sent for me." So Cornelius said, " Four days ago from this time, I was praying in my house at three o'clock in the afternoon, and, look you, a man stood before me in shining clothes and said, ' Cornelius, your prayer has been heard and your deeds of charity have been remembered before God. Send therefore to Joppa and send for Simon who is also called Peter. He is lodging in the house of Simon, a tanner, on the sea-shore.' Immediately I sent to you ; and I am most grateful that you have come. Now then we are all present before God to hear all that God has enjoined you to tell."

IN this passage the most surprising things are happening. Once again let us remember the Jewish attitude to the Gentiles. The Jew believed that for the Jews alone God had any use and that other nations were quite outside the mercy and the privileges of God. The really strict Jew would have no contact with a Gentile or even with a Jew who did not observe the Law. Two things in particular the strict Jew would not do. He would never have as a guest, nor would he ever be the guest of, a man who did not observe the Law. Remembering that, see what Peter did. When the emissaries of Cornelius were at the door—and note that, knowing the Jewish outlook, they came no farther than the door—Peter asked them in and gave them hospitality (verse 23). When Peter arrived at Caesarea, Cornelius met him at the door, no doubt wondering if Peter would cross his threshold at all, and Peter came in (verse 27). In the most amazing way the barriers are beginning to go down. Now that is typical of the work of Christ. A modern missionary tells how once he officiated at a communion service in Africa. Beside him as an elder there sat an old chief of the Ngoni called Manly-heart. And there were many Ngoni in the congregation. The old chief could remember the days when the young warriors of the Ngoni had gone out to blood their spears and had left behind them a trail of burned and devastated towns and had come home with their spears red with blood and with the women of their enemies as their booty. And what were the tribes which in those days they had ravaged ? They were the Senga and the Tumbuka. And who were sitting at that communion service now ? Ngoni, Senga and Tumbuka were sitting side by side, their enmities forgotten, one in the love of Jesus Christ. In the first days it was characteristic of Christianity that it broke the barriers down ; and Christianity can still do that when it gets the chance to do so.

THE HEART OF THE GOSPEL

Acts 10 : 34-43

> So Peter opened his mouth and said, " In truth I have come to understand that God has no favourites ; but that in every nation he who fears Him and acts righteously is acceptable to Him. As for the word which God sent to the sons of Israel, telling the good news of peace through Jesus Christ—this is He who is Lord of all—you all know the affair that happened all over Judaea, after the baptism which John preached —you know about Jesus of Nazareth, about how God anointed Him with the Spirit and with power, about how He went about healing all who were under the sway of the devil because God was with Him ; we are witnesses of all He did in the country of the Jews and in Jerusalem. And they took Him and hanged Him on a tree. It was He whom God raised up on the third day and made Him evident, not to all the people but to the witnesses elected beforehand by God, to us who were with Him and who ate with Him and drank with Him after He rose from the dead. And He gave us orders to preach to the people and to testify that this is He who was set apart by God, to be the judge of the living and the dead. To Him all the prophets testify—that everyone who believes in Him receives forgiveness of sins through His name."

IT is clear that we have here but the barest summary of what Peter said to Cornelius. Because of that it is all the more important because here we have the very essence of the first preaching about Jesus. (i) Jesus was sent by God and equipped by God with the Spirit and with power. Jesus therefore is God's gift to men. Often we make the mistake of thinking in terms of an angry God who had to be pacified by something a gentle Jesus did. The early preachers never preached that. To them the very coming

of Jesus was due to the love of God. (ii) Jesus exercised
a ministry of healing. He was uniquely the helper of men.
It was His great desire to banish all pain and sorrow from
the world. (iii) They took Him and they crucified Him.
Once again there is stressed for him who can read between
the lines the sheer horror of crime that was in the Crucifixion. That is what men's sin and disobedience can do.
(iv) He rose again. The power which sent Jesus and which
was in Jesus was a power not to be defeated. It could
conquer the worst that men could do and in the end it
could conquer death. (v) The Christian preacher and
teacher is a witness of the Resurrection. To him Jesus is
not a figure in a book or someone about whom he has heard.
He is a living presence whom he has met and with whom
he has spoken face to face. (vi) The result of all this is
forgiveness of sins. The result is that man has entered
into a new relationship with God. The estrangement,
the hostility, the fear are gone. Through Jesus the friendship which should always have existed between man and
God, but which sin interrupted, has dawned upon mankind.

THE ENTRY OF THE GENTILES

Acts 10 : 44-48

> When Peter was still saying these things the Holy
> Spirit fell upon those who were listening to his word.
> All the Jewish believers who had come with Peter
> were amazed that the gift of the Spirit had been
> poured out on the Gentiles too, for they heard them
> speaking with tongues and magnifying God. Then
> Peter said, " Can anyone stop water being brought ?
> Can anyone stop those who have received the Holy
> Spirit, as we too received Him, from being baptized? "
> And he ordered them to be baptized in the name of
> Jesus. Then they asked him to wait with them for
> some days.

EVEN as Peter was speaking things began to happen against
which even the Jewish Christians could not argue. The

Spirit came upon Cornelius and his friends. They were lifted out of themselves in an ecstasy and began to speak with tongues. This to the Jews was the final proof of the astonishing fact that God had given His Spirit to the Gentiles too. There are two interesting sidelights in this passage. (i) These Gentile converts, as always in Acts, were baptized there and then. In Acts there is no trace of one set of people only being able to administer baptism. Nowadays only an ordained minister of the Church can do so. The great truth in Acts was that it was the Christian Church as a Church which was receiving these converts. We would do well to remember in modern baptism that it is not the minister who is receiving a child, still less is he merely putting the child's name upon him ; it is the *Church* which is receiving the child on behalf of Jesus Christ. The Church would do well to remember that in every baptismal ceremony she is accepting responsibility for the child brought to her fellowship. (ii) The very last phrase is very significant. They asked Peter to wait with them for some days. Why ? Surely in order that he might teach them more and that they might learn more. We would do well to remember that the taking upon ourselves of Church membership is not the end of the road but the beginning of the road. There still remains the duty of learning, of penetrating more deeply every day into the unsearchable riches of Christ.

PETER ON HIS DEFENCE

Acts 11 : 1-10

> The apostles and the brethren who were throughout Judaea heard that the Gentiles too had received the word of God. So when Peter came up to Jerusalem those of the circumcision criticised him because, they said, " You went in to men who had never been circumcised and you ate with them." So Peter began at the beginning and told them the whole story. He said, " I was praying in the city of Joppa ; in a trance

I saw a vision. I saw a kind of vessel coming **down like** a great sheet let down by the four corners from heaven ; and it came right down to me. I was gazing at it and trying to make out what it was and I saw on it the four-footed beasts of the earth and the wild beasts and the creeping animals and the animals that fly in the air. And I heard a voice saying to me, ' Rise, Peter, kill and eat.' I said, ' By no means, Lord, because food which is common or unclean has never entered my mouth.' Again the voice spoke from heaven, ' What God has cleansed do not you reckon as common.' This happened three times ; and they were all drawn up into heaven again."

THE importance that Luke attached to this incident is shown by the amount of space that he devoted to it. In ancient times a writer had by no means unlimited space. At this time the book form had not come into use. Writers used rolls of a material called papyrus, which was the forerunner of paper and which was made of the pith of the papyrus plant, which is a kind of bulrush. Now a roll is an unwieldy thing and the length which could be conveniently handled was strictly limited. The longest roll that was used was about thirty-five feet long and that would be almost precisely the length of a roll required to hold the book of Acts. Into that space Luke had almost endless material to fit. He must have selected with the greatest care what he was going to preserve and set down ; and yet he finds this incident of Peter and Cornelius of such paramount importance that he relates it in full twice. Luke was right. We usually do not realize how near Christianity was to becoming only another kind of Judaism. All the first Christians were Jews and the whole tradition and outlook of Judaism would have moved them to keep this new wonder to themselves and to believe that God could not possibly have meant it for the despised Gentiles. Luke gives us this incident in full twice over because he sees it as a notable mile-stone on the road along which the Church was groping its way to the conception of a world for Christ.

A CONVINCING STORY

Acts II : II-I8

"And, look you, thereupon, three men, who had been sent to me from Caesarea, stood at the house where we were. The Spirit told me to go with them and to make no distinctions. These six brethren also came with me and we came to the man's house. He told us how in the house he had seen the angel standing and saying, ' Send to Joppa and send for Simon, who is also called Peter, who will speak words to you by which you and all your house will be saved.' As I was beginning to speak, the Holy Spirit fell upon them, just as in the beginning He did upon you. And I remembered the Lord's word and how He said, ' John baptized you with water, but you will be baptized with the Holy Spirit.' If God gave the same gift to them as to us who have believed in the Lord Jesus Christ, who was I to be able to hinder God?" When they heard this they had no protests to make and they glorified God saying, " So God has given life-giving repentance to the Gentiles too."

THE fault for which Peter was initially on trial was that he had gone in and had eaten with Gentiles (verse 3). We have already seen that a strict Jew would have no converse with a Gentile. It was barely conceivable that for some practical purpose a Jew might have entered a Gentile house, although even that was very unlikely ; but it was utterly incredible that he should have sat at meat with them. By eating with these Gentiles, Peter had outraged the ancestral Law and traditions of his people. Now we must note Peter's defence. Peter's defence was not an argument ; it was a statement of the facts. Whatever these critics might say the Holy Spirit had come upon these Gentiles in the most notable way. On that there was no argument. In verse I2 there is an interesting and significant sidelight. Peter says that he took six brethren with him. Together with himself that made seven persons present. In Egyptian law, which the Jews would know well, seven witnesses were necessary completely to prove a case. In Roman law, which they would also know well, seven seals were necessary to authenticate a really important document like a will. So Peter is in effect saying, " I am not arguing with you. I am telling you the facts and of these facts there are seven witnesses. The case is proved." The proof of Christianity always lies in facts. It is very doubtful if anyone has ever been argued into Christianity by verbal proofs and logical demonstrations. The proof of Christianity is that it works, that it does in point of fact change men, that it does make bad men good, that it does bring to men the Spirit of God ; and therefore the duty of the Christian is not to talk about his faith but to demonstrate his faith. It is when a man's deeds give the lie to his words that the gravest discredit is brought on Christianity ; it is when a man's words are guaranteed by his deeds that the world is presented with an argument for Christianity which will brook no denial.

GREAT THINGS IN ANTIOCH

Acts II : 19-21

> Those who had been dispersed by the persecution following upon the death of Stephen went through the country as far as Phoenicia and Cyprus and Antioch, but they spoke the word to no one except to Jews. But some of them, men from Cyprus and Cyrene, came to Antioch and spoke to the Greeks too and told them the good news of the Lord Jesus. The Lord's hand was with them ; and a great number believed and turned to the Lord.

IN their sober and restrained sentences these few words tell of one of the greatest events in history. Now, for the first time, the gospel is deliberately preached to the Gentiles. Everything has been working up to this. There have been three steps on the ladder and three mile-stones on the way. First, Philip preached to the Samaritans. That was **one step** ; but the Samaritans after all were half Jewish and they formed, as it were, a bridge, between the Jewish and the Gentile world. Second, Peter had accepted Cornelius. But note, in the case of Cornelius there was one vital difference. It was Cornelius who had taken the initiative. It was not the Christian Church who sought Cornelius ; it was Cornelius who sought the Christian Church. Further, it is stressed that Cornelius was a God-fearer and, therefore, he was, as it were, on the fringes of the Jewish faith. Third, now in Antioch we have the last and final step. For there the Church did not go to people who were Jews or half Jews ; nor did it wait to be approached by Gentiles seeking admission. Deliberately and of set purpose, spontaneously and without waiting for the invitation, it preached the gospel to the Gentiles. Christianity is finally launched on its world-wide mission.

Here we have a truly amazing thing. The Church has taken the most epoch-making of all steps ; and we do not even know the names of the people who took that step. All we know is that they came from Cyprus and Cyrene ; but who they were no man knows and no man will ever know. They go down to history as the nameless pioneers of Christ. It has always been one of the tragedies of the Church that men have wished to be noticed, named, thanked, praised when they did something which they thought worth while. What the Church has always needed, perhaps more than anything else, is people who will do the work and never care who gains the credit for it, so be it that the work is done. These men may never have written their name in men's books of history ; but they wrote them forever in the Book of Life.

But there emerges another amazing fact. This incident begins a section of Acts where Antioch occupies the centre of the stage. Antioch was the third greatest city in the world. Only Rome and Alexandria surpassed her. She stood near the mouth of the river Orontes, fifteen miles from the Mediterranean Sea. She was a lovely city and she was a cosmopolitan city. But she was a byword for luxurious immorality. She was famous for her chariot-racing and for a kind of deliberate pursuit of pleasure which went on literally night and day. To put it in modern terms, we might describe her as a city of sport run mad, of betting and gambling and night clubs. But most of all she was famous for the worship of Daphne whose temple stood five miles out of the town amidst its laurel groves. The legend was that Daphne was a mortal maid with whom Apollo fell in love. He pursued her, and to save her Daphne was changed into a laurel bush. The priestesses of the Temple of Daphne were sacred prostitutes and, nightly, in these laurel groves the pursuit was re-enacted by the worshippers and the priestesses. " The morals of Daphne " was a phrase that all the world knew for loose and lustful living. It seems incredible but nonetheless it is true that it was in a city like that that Christianity took the great stride forward to becoming the religion of the world. We have only to think of that to discover there is no such thing as a hopeless situation.

THE WISDOM OF BARNABAS

Acts II : 22-26

> News of this and of what they were doing came to the ears of the Church in Jerusalem. So they sent Barnabas out as far as Antioch. When he came and saw the grace of God he was glad and he exhorted them all to make it the set purpose of their hearts to cleave to the Lord, for he was a good man and full of the Holy Spirit and of faith. He went away to Tarsus to look for Saul and when he had found him he brought him to Antioch. For a whole year they were guests of the Church there and they instructed a very considerable number of people. And it was at Antioch that the disciples first received the name of Christians.

WHEN the leaders of the Church at Jerusalem got word of what was going on at Antioch they very naturally sent down to investigate the situation.

It was by the grace of God they sent the man they did send. They might have sent someone of a rigid and a narrow mind who had made a god of the Law and who was shackled by its rules and regulations ; but they sent the man with the biggest heart in the Church. They sent Barnabas. Barnabas had already stood by Paul and sponsored him when all men suspected him (Acts 9 : 27). Barnabas had already given proof of his Christian love by his generosity to his needy brethren (Acts 4 : 36, 37). So when Barnabas came down to see what was happening, and when he saw the Gentiles being swept into the fellowship of the Church he was glad. But someone must be found to be put in charge of this work. That someone must be a man who had a double background. He must be a Jew brought up in the Jewish tradition ; but he must also be a man who could meet the Gentiles on equal terms. He must be a man of courage, for Antioch was no easy place to be a Christian leader ; and he must be a man of skill in words and arguments to meet the double attack of Jews and Gentiles on the Church. Barnabas knew the very man. For nine years or thereby we have heard nothing of Paul. The last glimpse we had of him he was escaping by way of Caesarea to Tarsus (Acts 9 : 30). No doubt for nine years he had been witnessing for Christ in his native town. He had been preparing himself, and now the task for which he had been destined was ready for him ; and Barnabas with a profound wisdom put him in charge of it.

It was in Antioch that the Christians were first called Christians. The word Christian began by being a nickname. The people of Antioch were famous for their facility in finding jesting nicknames. Later the bearded Emperor Julian came to visit him and they christened him " The Goat." The termination *-iani* means *belonging to the party of.* For instance *Caesariani* means *belonging to Caesar's party.* Christians means *These Christ-folk.* It was a half-mocking half-jesting, wholly contemptuous nickname. But the Christians took that nickname and made it a name which

all the world was to know. By their lives they made it
a name not of contempt but at the courage and love of
which all men were to wonder.

HELPING IN TROUBLE

Acts II : 27-30

> In these days prophets came down from Jerusalem
> to Antioch. One of them called Agabus stood up and,
> through the Holy Spirit, gave them a sign that a
> great famine was to come upon the whole land. This
> happened in the reign of Claudius. But each of the
> disciples, in proportion to his resources, fixed upon
> an amount for a relief fund to send to the brethren
> who lived in Judaea. This they did and despatched
> it to the elders through the hand of Barnabas and Saul.

HERE the prophets come upon the scene. In the Early
Church they were very important people. They are
mentioned again in Acts 13 : 1 ; 15 : 32 ; 21 : 9, 10.
In the Early Church, broadly speaking, there were three
sets of leaders and officials. (i) There were the *Apostles*.
Their authority was not confined to one place ; their
writ ran throughout the whole Church ; they were looked
upon as being in a very real sense the successors of Jesus.
(ii) There were the *Elders*. The elders were the local
officials. Their authority was confined to the place where
they were set apart. They were the local officials of the
local Churches. (iii) There were the *Prophets*. Their
function is to be seen in their name. The word *prophet*
means both a *fore-teller* and a *forth-teller*. They were men
who foretold the future ; but even more they were men
who forthtold the will of God. They had no settled sphere ;
they were not attached to any one Church. They were
men who lived close to God and who had no homes and
no ties but who went everywhere pointing men to God.
They were held in the highest honour. *The Teaching of
the Twelve Apostles* which dates to about 100 A.D., contains

the first service order book of the Church. The order for the Eucharist service, the sacrament of the Lord's Supper, is laid down, but then it is said that the prophets are to be allowed to conduct the service as they will. Men knew that they had special gifts. But they had special dangers too. The career of prophet was a career which a man might undertake not from the highest but the lowest of motives. The false prophet existed, the man who simply battened on the charity of the Church and lived on charity. The same *Teaching of the Twelve Apostles* warns against the prophet who in a vision asks for money or for a meal ; it instructs that prophets should always be given hospitality for one night but if they desire to stay longer without working they are false prophets. The prophets were the wandering men of God of the Early Church.

This whole incident is very significant for it shows that thus early men had realised the unity of the Church. If there was famine in Palestine the first instinct of the Church at Antioch was to help. They knew in those days that they were all members of the body of Christ. To them it was unthinkable that one part of the Church should be in trouble and that another should do nothing about it. They were still far from the congregational outlook ; they had that width of vision which saw the Church as a whole. They were not members of the Church of Antioch ; they were members of the Church of Christ.

IMPRISONMENT AND DELIVERANCE

Acts 12 : 1-11

> About this time Herod the king began to take hostile action to inflict injury on certain men of the Church. He killed James, John's brother, with the sword. When he saw that this gave pleasure to the Jews he went to arrest Peter too. (These were the days of unleavened bread). When he had seized Peter, he put him under arrest. He handed him over to four

squads of soldiers to guard, for he wished to bring him before the people after the Passover Feast. So Peter was continuously guarded in prison. Prayer to God for him was earnestly offered by the Church. On the night before Herod was going to bring him before the people, Peter was sleeping between two soldiers, bound by two chains ; and guards kept continuous watch before the door. Now, look you, the Angel of the Lord stood by and a light shone in the house. He struck Peter's side and wakened him and said, " Rise quickly." The chains fell from his hands. The angel said to him, " Gird yourself and put on your sandals." He did so. He said to him, " Wrap your cloak round about you and follow me." So he went out and followed him. And he did not know that what was happening through the angel was real, but he thought that he was seeing a vision. They went through the first and the second guard and they came to the iron door that led into the city and it opened to them of its own accord. They went out and they proceeded along one street ; and thereupon the angel left him. When Peter had recovered his faculties he said, " Now I know for sure that the Lord sent his angel and delivered me from the hand of Herod and rescued me from the fate that the people of the Jews looked forward to for me."

THERE now broke out upon the Church, and especially upon its leaders, a new wave of persecution. Behind this persecution there was the influence of King Herod. Let us see briefly the various ramifications of the family of the Herods in their New Testament connections. The first of the New Testament Herods is *Herod the Great.* He was in power from about 41 B.C. to 1 B.C. He is the Herod of Matthew 2, who was in power when Jesus was born, who received the Wise Men from the East and who massacred the children. Herod the Great was married ten times. Of his family those who cross the pages of the New Testament are :—(i) *Herod Philip the First.* He was the first husband of Herodias who was responsible for the death of John the Baptist. He is mentioned, under the name of Philip, in Matthew 14 : 3 ; Mark 6 : 17 ; Luke 3 : 19. He had no official office. He was the father ɔf Salome. (ii) *Herod Antipas.* He was the ruler of Galilee and Peraea. He was the second husband of Herodias and consented to the death of John the Baptist. He was also the Herod to whom Pilate sent Jesus for trial (Luke 23 : 7ff). (iii) *Archelaus.* He was ruler of Judaea, Samaria and Idumaea. He was a thoroughly bad ruler and was deposed and banished. He is mentioned in Matthew 2 : 22. (iv) *Herod Philip the Second.* He was ruler of Ituraea and Trachonitis. He was the founder of Caesarea Philippi which was called after him. In the New Testament he is called Philip and is mentioned in Luke 3 : 1. (v) Herod the Great had another son called Aristobulus ; his mother was Mariamne, a princess who was descended from the great Maccabaean heroes. He was murdered by his own father but he had a son called *Herod Agrippa.* This is the Herod of our present passage in Acts 12. (vi) To complete the list we may note that this Herod Agrippa was the father of (a) *Agrippa the Second* before whom Paul was examined and before whom Paul made his famous speech (Acts 25 and 26). (b) *Bernice* who appears with him when Paul was under examination. (c) *Drusilla* who was the wife of Felix, the governor before whom Paul was tried (Acts 24 : 24). From this family history it is seen that Herod Agrippa of this chapter was a direct descendant of the Maccabees through his mother Mariamne. He had been educated at Rome, but he sedulously cultivated the good graces of the Jewish people by meticulously keeping the Law and all Jewish observances. For these reasons he was popular with the people ; and it was no doubt in order to achieve further popularity with the orthodox Jews that he decided to take steps to attack the Christian Church and its leaders. It is therefore seen that James was the victim of Herod's schemes to win popular favour and that Peter's imprisonment was due to the same scheme. Even his conduct in the arrest of Peter shows his desire to conciliate the Jews. The Passover Feast was on 14th Nisan ; for that day and the seven following days no leaven must be used ; that week was called the days of unleavened bread. During that week no trial or execution could be carried out and that is why Herod purposed to defer Peter's execution until the week was finished. The great tragedy of this particular wave of persecution was that it was not due to any man's principles, however misguided ; it was simply due to Herod's bid to gain the popular favour of the people.

THE JOY OF RESTORATION

Acts 12 : 12-19

> When Peter had grasped what had happened, he went to the house of Mary, the mother of John, who was surnamed Mark. There a large number had assembled together and were praying. When Peter had knocked at the door of the entrance a maid-servant called Rhoda came to answer the door. She recognized Peter's voice, and, in her joy, she did not open the door but ran and told them that Peter stood before the entrance. They said to her, " You are mad." She strenuously insisted that it was so ; but they kept saying, " It is his angel." But Peter waited there knocking. When they opened the door and saw him they were amazed. With a gesture of his hand he bade them be silent, and he told them the whole story of how the Lord had brought him out of prison. He said, " Tell these tidings to James and to the brethren." So he went away to another place. When day came there was no small disturbance among the soldiers about what had happened to Peter. When Herod had sought for him and did not find him, he examined the guards and ordered them to be led away to execution. And he went down from Judaea to Caesarea and stayed there.

THE greatest precautions had been taken to see that Peter did not escape. He was guarded by four quaternions of soldiers. A quaternion was a squad of four. There were four such squads because the day and the night were divided into four watches each of three hours duration ;

and each squad was on duty for three hours at a time. Normally a prisoner was chained by his right hand to his guard's left hand ; but Peter was chained by both hands to a guard on each side of him, while the two remaining soldiers of the quaternion on duty kept watch at the door. Precautions could go no further. When Peter did escape the soldiers were led away to execution because it was the law that, if a criminal escaped, his guard should suffer the same penalty as the prisoner would have suffered.

In this story we do not necessarily need to see a miracle. It may well be the story of a thrilling rescue and escape. Even if it were such it would still have been told in the same terms because, however it happened, the hand of God was most definitely in it.

When Peter escaped he took his way straight to the house of Mary, the mother of John Mark. From that we would learn that the headquarters of the Christian Church was there. It has indeed been suggested that it was in that very house that the Last Supper had been eaten and that it had continued to be the meeting place of the disciples in Jerusalem. We may well note what the Christians were doing in that house. They were praying. When they were up against it and when they had nowhere else to go they went to God.

In this passage we come on the first mention of the man who was the real leader of the Christian Church in Jerusalem. Peter instructs them to go and to tell the news to James. This James is James the brother of our Lord. Now there is a certain mystery about this James. In the East it would have been the natural and the accepted thing for the next brother to take on the work and the task of an elder brother who had been killed ; but from the story of the gospels we learn that Jesus' brothers did not believe in him (John 7 : 5) and that they actually thought him mad (Mark 3 : 21). During His lifetime James was not a supporter of Jesus. But we learn that the Risen Christ made a special resurrection appearance to

James (I Corinthians 15 : 7). There is a very ancient gospel called the Gospel according to the Hebrews which tells how after the death of Jesus, James made a vow that he would neither eat nor drink until he saw Jesus again ; and that Jesus did appear to him. It may well be that what the life of Jesus could not do His death did do, and that when James saw his brother die he discovered who He really was and dedicated all his life to serve Him. The change in James may well be another great example of the power of the Cross to change the lives of men.

A TERRIBLE END

Acts 12 : 20-25

Herod was furious with the people of Tyre and Sidon. But they came to him with a common purpose. They gained the ear of Blastus the king's chamberlain and sued for peace because their country was dependent for its sustenance on the king's territory. Upon an agreed day Herod put on his royal robes and seated himself on a throne and made a speech to them. The people cried out, " It is the voice of a God and not of a man." Immediately the angel of the Lord struck him because he did not give the glory to God. And he was eaten with worms and died.

The word of God increased and was multiplied. And Barnabas and Saul returned from Jerusalem, when they had completed their errand of mercy, and they took with them John who was surnamed Mark.

HERE we read of the terrible end which, with a kind of poetic justice, fell upon Herod. There was at this time some quarrel between him and the people of Tyre and Sidon. For these peoples this quarrel was a serious matter. Their lands lay to the North of Palestine. In two ways Herod could make things very difficult for them. If he deflected the trade of Palestine from their ports their revenues would be seriously impaired. And worse, Tyre and Sidon were dependent for their food supplies on

Palestine and if these supplies were cut off their case would be serious indeed. These people succeeded in gaining the ear of Blastus, the king's chamberlain. In due course a public session was arranged. We have to remember Herod's popularity with the people. Josephus, the Jewish historian, describes how, on the second day of the festival, he entered the theatre clad in a robe of silver cloth. The sun glinted on the silver and the people cried out that this was a god come to them. Thereupon a sudden and a terrible illness fell upon him from which he never recovered. The pride of man had ended in the wrath of God.

Verses 24 and 25 take us back to Acts 11 : 27-30. Paul and Barnabas had fulfilled their errand of mercy to the Church at Jerusalem and so returned to Antioch, taking with them John Mark.

THE FIRST MISSIONARY JOURNEY

The 13th and 14th chapters of Acts tell the story of the First Missionary Journey. Paul and Barnabas set out from Antioch. Antioch was 15 miles up the River Orontes so they actually sailed from Seleucia which was the port of Antioch. From there they went across the sea to Cyprus. In Cyprus they preached at Salamis and Paphos. They sailed from Paphos and landed at Perga in Pamphylia. Pamphylia was a low-lying coastal province. They did not preach there. As we shall see, the reason why they did not preach was that the low-lying coastal strip did not suit Paul's health. They struck inland and came to Antioch in Pisidia. When things grew too dangerous there they went still further on to Iconium which was about 90 miles from Antioch. Once again their lives were threatened and they moved on to Lystra which was about 20 miles away. After suffering a very serious and dangerous attack there they passed on to Derbe, the site of which has not yet been definitely identified. From Derbe they set out on the way home, going back to Lystra, Iconium and Antioch in Pisidia. From there they made their way down to the coastal province of Pamphylia. This time they preached in Perga. Then they took ship from Attalia which was the principal port of Pamphylia and sailed to Seleucia and so back to Antioch. The whole journey occupied a period of about three years.

SENT OUT BY THE HOLY SPIRIT

Acts 13 : 1-3

> In the local Church at Antioch there were prophets and teachers. There were Barnabas, and Simeon who is called Niger, and Lucius from Cyrene, and Manaen, who was brought up with Herod the tetrarch, and Saul. When they were engaged in worshipping God and in fasting, the Holy Spirit said to them, " Come now, set apart for Me Barnabas and Saul for the work to which I have called them in My service." So after they had fasted and prayed they laid their hands on them and let them go.

THE Christian Church was now poised to take the greatest of all steps. They had decided, quite deliberately, to take the message of the gospel out to all the world. It was a step which was taken under the direct guidance of the Holy Spirit. It was always true of the men of the Early Church that they never did what they wanted to do, but always what God wanted them to do.

The passage speaks of *prophets* and *teachers*. The prophets and the teachers had different functions. The prophets were not attached to any one Church. They were wandering preachers who had given their whole lives to listening for the word of God then taking that word to their fellow men. The teachers were the men in the local Churches whose duty it was to instruct those who came into Christianity in the faith.

It has been pointed out that this very list of prophets is symbolic of the universal appeal of the Gospel. Barnabas was a Jew from Cyprus ; Lucius came from Cyrene in North Africa ; Simeon was also a Jew but his other name Niger is given and that is a Roman name and shows that he must have moved in Roman circles ; Manaen was a man with aristocratic and courtly connections ; and Paul himself was a Jew from Tarsus in Cilicia and a trained Rabbi. There in that little band there is exemplified the unifying influence of Christianity. Men from many lands and many backgrounds had discovered the secret of " togetherness " because they had discovered the secret of Christ.

One extremely interesting speculation has been made. Simeon who was also called Niger not improbably came from Africa, for Niger is an African name. It has been suggested that this very Simeon is the same man as Simon of Cyrene who carried Jesus' Cross (Luke 23 : 26). It would be a thing most wonderful if the man whose first contact with Jesus was the carrying of the Cross—a task which he must have bitterly resented—was one of the men mainly and directly responsible for sending out the story of the Cross to all the world.

SUCCESS IN CYPRUS

Acts 13 : 4-12

So when they had been sent out by the Holy Spirit they went down to Seleucia, and from there they sailed away to Cyprus. When they were in Salamis they proclaimed the word of God in the Synagogue of the Jews ; and they had John as their helper. They went through the whole island as far as Paphos ; and there they found a man who was a dealer in magic, a false prophet and a Jew. His name was Bar-Jesus and he was with the pro-consul Sergius Paulus who was an intelligent man. The pro-consul summoned Barnabas and Saul and sought to hear the word of God. Elymas (for such is the translation of his name), the man of magic, opposed them and tried to turn the pro-consul away from the faith. But Saul—who is also Paul—filled with the Holy Spirit, fixed his gaze upon him and said, " You who are full of all deceit and all villainy, you son of the devil, you enemy of righteousness, will you not stop twisting the straight ways of God ? And now, look you, the Lord's hand is on you and you will be blind and you will not see the sun for a season." And thereupon a mist and a darkness fell upon him ; and as he groped about he looked for people to lead him by the hand. When the pro-consul saw what had happened, in astonishment, he believed in the teaching of the Lord.

It was to Cyprus that Paul and Barnabas first went. We may see the hand of Barnabas there. He was a native of Cyprus (Acts 4 : 36), and it would be typical of the gracious heart of Barnabas that he desired to share the treasures of Jesus first of all with his own people. Cyprus was a Roman province. It was famous for its copper mines and its shipbuilding industry. It was sometimes called Makaria which means the Happy Isle, because it was held that its climate was so perfect and its resources and products so varied that a man might find everything necessary for a happy life within its bounds. Paul never chose an easy way. He and Barnabas preached in Paphos, the capital of the island. Paphos was famous or infamous for the worship of Venus, the goddess of love, and was a byword for lustful immorality. The governor of Cyprus was Sergius Paulus. These were intensely superstitious times. Superstition is always the sign of a decadent civilisation. Most great men, even an intelligent man like Sergius Paulus, kept private wizards, who were sooth-sayers and fortune tellers and who dealt in magic and spells. Bar-Jesus, or Elymas—an Arabic word which means *the skilful one*—was the private wizard of Sergius Paulus. He saw that if the governor was won for Christianity his day was done. But Paul dealt effectively with him.

Up to this time in Acts Paul is called Saul. In those days nearly all Jews had two names. One was a Jewish name, by which they were known in their own circle ; the other was a Greek name, by which they were known in the wider world. It is so, for instance, in the Highlands to this day, where James may be Hamish and John may be Ian at home. Sometimes the Greek name translated the Hebrew name. So Cephas is the Hebrew and Peter the Greek for a rock ; so Thomas is the Hebrew and Didymus the Greek for a twin. Sometimes it echoed the sound. So Eliakim in Hebrew becomes Alcimus in Greek and so Joshua becomes Jesus. So Paul was Saul, his Hebrew name, at home and Paul in the wider world. It may well be that from this time he so fully accepted his mission as the apostle to the Gentiles that he determined to use only his Gentile name. If so, it was the mark that from this time he was launched on the career for which the Holy Spirit had marked him out and that there was no turning back.

THE DESERTER

Acts 13 : 13

> Paul and his friends put out to sea from Paphos and came to Perga in Pamphylia ; and John left them and went back to Jerusalem.

WITHOUT his name even being mentioned this verse pays the greatest of all tributes to Barnabas. Up to this time the order has always been Barnabas and Saul (Acts 13 : 2). It was Barnabas who had set out as the leader of this expedition. But now it is Paul and Barnabas. In the very nature of things it is Paul who has assumed the leadership of the expedition. And the lovely thing about Barnabas is that there is from him no word of complaint. He was a man prepared to take the second place, so be it God's work was done.

But the main interest of this verse is that it is a strand in the biography of John Mark—for the John mentioned here is the man we know better as Mark—who was at one and the same time the deserter and the man who redeemed himself. Mark was very young. His mother's house seems to have been the centre of the Church at Jerusalem (Acts 12 : 12) and Mark must always have been very close to the centre of the faith. Paul and Barnabas took him with them as their helper, for he was the kinsman of Barnabas ; and now he turned and went home. We will never know why. Perhaps he resented the deposition of Barnabas from the leadership ; perhaps he was afraid of the proposed journey up into the plateau where Antioch in Pisidia stood for it was one of the hardest and most dangerous roads in the world ; perhaps, because he came from Jerusalem, he had his doubts about this preaching to the Gentiles ; perhaps at this stage he was one of these lads who was better at beginning things than finishing them ; perhaps—as Chrysostom said long ago—the lad wanted his mother. However it was he went. For a time Paul found it hard to forgive. When he set out on the second missionary journey Barnabas wanted to take Mark again but Paul refused to take the lad who had played the deserter in Pamphylia (Acts 15 : 38) and Paul and Barnabas split company for good over this. Then Mark vanishes from history. Tradition and legend say he went to Alexandria and Egypt and founded the Church there. But when he re-emerges almost 20 years later he is the man who has redeemed himself. When Paul wrote to the Colossians when he was in prison in Rome he tells them to receive Mark if he comes to them. So Mark is with Paul again. And at the very end when he wrote to Timothy just before his death he says, " Take Mark and bring him with you, for he is a useful man when it comes to doing a bit of service " (2 Timothy 4 : 11). The man who was once a deserter has become the man who was useful to Paul. As Fosdick put it, " No man need stay the way he is." By the grace of God the man who was the deserter became the writer of a gospel and the man whom, at the end, Paul wanted with him.

AN ADVENTUROUS JOURNEY FOR A SICK MAN

Acts 13 : 14, 15

> From Perga they went through the country and
> arrived at Pisidian Antioch. They went into the
> Synagogue on the first day of the week and sat down.
> After the reading of the Law and the Prophets the
> rulers of the Synagogue sent to them with this message,
> " Brothers, if you have any word of exhortation to
> say to the people say on."

ONE of the amazing things about Acts is the heroism
that is passed over in a sentence. Pisidian Antioch stood
on a plateau 3,600 feet above sea-level. To get to it Paul
and Barnabas would have to cross the Taurus range of
mountains by one of the hardest roads in Asia Minor,
a road which was also notorious for robbers and brigands.
They were setting out on one of the most dangerous of
all journeys. But we are bound to ask the question, why
did they not preach in Pamphylia ? Why did they leave
the coast with the word unproclaimed and set out on that
difficult and dangerous way ? Not so very long afterwards
Paul wrote a letter to the people of Antioch in Pisidia,
Iconium, Lystra and Derbe. It is the letter called the
Letter to the Galatians for all these towns were in the
Roman province of Galatia. In that letter he says something. " You know that it was because I was sick in body
that I first brought the good news to you " (Galatians
4 : 13). So when he came to Galatia he was a sick man.
Now all men know that Paul had a thorn in the flesh
which in spite of much prayer remained with him (2
Corinthians 12 : 7, 8). Many guesses have been made as to
what that thorn—or *stake* as it more likely should be
translated—was. The oldest tradition is that Paul suffered
from prostrating headaches. And the most likely explanation is that he was the victim of a virulent recurring
malaria fever which haunted the low coastal strip of Asia
Minor. A traveller says that the headache characteristic
of this malaria was like a red-hot bar thrust through

the forehead ; and another likens it to a dentist's drill boring through a man's temple. It is most likely that this malaria attacked Paul in low-lying Pamphylia and that he had to make for the plateau country to shake it off. Now note, it never struck him to turn back. It was a sick man who faced that grim journey up through the hills. Even when his body was aching Paul never ceased to drive on and to be an adventurer for Christ. And so in these two verses there is a hidden romance of heroism for those who can see.

THE PREACHING OF PAUL

Acts 13 : 16-41

Then Paul stood up and made a gesture with his hand and said, " You Israelites, and you who are God-fearers, listen to this. The God of this people Israel chose out our fathers and He exalted the people when they lived as strangers in the land of Egypt, and with a lofty arm He brought them forth from it. For forty years He bore with their ways in the wilderness. He destroyed seven nations in the land of Canaan and gave them possession of their land, for about four hundred and fifty years. After that He gave them judges up to the time of Samuel the prophet. Thereafter they asked for a king. And God gave them Saul, the son of Kish, a man of the tribe of Benjamin for forty years. God removed him and raised up David as king for them. In testimony to him He said, ' I found in David, the son of Jesse, a man after My own heart, who will do all things that I wish.' It was from the seed of this man, according to His promise, that God brought Jesus, a Saviour for Israel, after John had previously preached, before His coming, a baptism of repentance to all the people of Israel. When John was fulfilling his course, he said, ' What do you suppose me to be ? No. I am not He. But, look you, there is coming after me one the shoe of whose feet I am not fit to unloose.' Brethren, you who are sons of the race of Abraham, you God-fearers among us, it was for us that the word of this salvation was sent out. Those who live in Jerusalem and their rulers did not recognize this man and they fulfilled the words of the prophets which are read every Sabbath when they condemned Him in judgment. Though they found in Him no charge which merited the death penalty, they asked Pilate that He should be put to death. When they had completed all that had been written about Him they took Him down from the tree and put Him in a tomb. But God raised Him from the dead and He was seen for many days by those who had come up with Him from Galilee to Jerusalem, and they are now witnesses of Him to the people ; and we bring you the good news of that promise, that was made to the fathers ; we tell you that God has fulfilled this to our children by raising up Jesus, even as it stands written in the second psalm, ' Thou art My son ; this day have I begotten thee.' And when He raised Him from the dead no longer to return to destruction He spoke thus, ' I will give to you the holy things of David which are faithful,' because He says in another passage, ' Thou wilt not allow Thy holy one to see corruption.' For David in his own generation served the will of God and fell asleep, and he was added to his fathers and he *did* see corruption. But the one whom God raised up did not see corruption. Let this be known to you, brethren, that through this man the forgiveness of sins is proclaimed to us. And from all the things from which you could not be acquitted by the Law of Moses, everyone who believes in this man is acquitted. So then, take heed lest there come upon you that which was spoken in the prophets—' See, you despisers, and wonder, and be wiped out from sight, because I work a work in your days, a work in which you will not believe, even if someone tell it to you.'"

THIS is an extremely interesting and important passage because it is the only full-length report of a sermon by Paul that we possess. It should be carefully compared with the sermon of Peter in Acts 2 ; and it will be seen that the main elements in it are precisely the same.

This sermon of Paul has five main points. (i) Paul insists that the coming of Jesus is the consummation of history. He outlines the national history of the Jews to show that it culminates in Christ. History is no purposeless process. The Stoics believed that history went in cycles, that every cycle the world was destroyed in a vast conflagration and that thereafter the same process started all over again. History to them simply kept on repeating itself. A modern cynical verdict is that history is the record of the sins, the mistakes and the follies of men. But the Christian view of history is characteristically optimistic. It is certain that always history is going somewhere according to the purpose of God. (ii) Paul states the fact that men did not recognize God's consummation when it came in Jesus Christ. Browning said, " We needs must love the highest when we see it." But a man, by taking his own way and refusing God's way, can in the end afflict himself with a blindness which is unable to see. The misuse of freewill ends not in liberty but in ruin. (iii) Although men, in their blind folly, rejected and crucified Jesus, God could not be defeated and the Resurrection is the proof of the undefeatable purpose and power of God. It is told that once on a stormy night when a gale was blowing, a child said in awe to his father, " God must have lost grip of His winds to-night." The Resurrection is the proof that God never loses grip, that in the end His purpose and His will reign supreme. (iv) Paul goes on to use a purely Jewish argument. The Resurrection is the fulfilment of prophecy because promises were made to David which were obviously not fulfilled in him but which are fulfilled in Christ. Now once again, however little we are prepared to make of the argument from prophecy nowadays, the fact remains that history is a forward-looking process. It is neither circular nor aimless ; it looks to that which in the purpose of God must come. (v) The coming and the message of Christ is to one kind of people good news. Hitherto they had lived life according to the Law. No man could ever fulfil the law completely and therefore any thinking man was always conscious of failure, inadequacy and inevitable guilt. But in Jesus Christ and in His life and death men find that liberating and that forgiving power which sets them free from the condemnation which should have been theirs, and which therefore restores real friendship and fellowship between God and man. (vi) But that which is meant for good news and which was designed as good news is in fact bad news for another kind of people. It simply makes worse the condemnation of those who in their blindness have seen it and who have neglected it and disobeyed its summons to belief in and acceptance of Jesus Christ. There is excuse for the man who has never had a chance ; but there is no excuse for the man who has seen the splendour of the offer of God and who has rejected it. That which is a gift of love to those who take it is a condemnation to those who refuse it.

TROUBLE AT ANTIOCH

Acts 13 : 42-52

As they were going out, they kept asking that these things should be spoken to them on the next Sabbath. When the Synagogue service had broken up many of the Jews and worshipping proselytes followed Paul and Barnabas. They talked with them and tried to persuade them to abide in the grace of God.

On the next Sabbath nearly the whole city assembled to hear the word of God. When the Jews saw the crowds they were filled with envy and they argued against what Paul said, making blasphemous statements. Paul and Barnabas, using the boldest language, said, " It was necessary that the word of God should first be spoken to you, but since you reject it and since you have proved that you are unfit for eternal life, look you, we turn to the Gentiles ; for thus has the Lord enjoined us, ' I have appointed you for a light to the Gentiles so that you may be for salvation even to the utmost bound of the world.' " When the Gentiles heard this they were glad and they glorified the word of God ; and all who were appointed to eternal life believed. And the word of the Lord was carried throughout the whole district. But the Jews incited the devout women who were women of position and the chief men of the city and raised persecution against Paul and Barnabas ; and they ejected them from their bounds. But they shook off the dust of their feet against them and went to Iconium. And the disciples were filled with joy and the Holy Spirit.

ANTIOCH in Pisidia was naturally an inflammable city. It was a very mixed place. It had been founded by one of Alexander the Great's successors about 300 B.C. Jews very often flooded into new cities in order to get in on the ground floor, in the modern phrase. Since Antioch was a road centre it had become a Roman Colony in 6 B.C. In the population there were therefore Greeks, Jews, Romans and not a few of the native Phrygians who were an emotional and unstable people. It was the kind of population where a spark could cause a conflagration. The one thing that infuriated the Jews was that any of God's privileges could be for the uncircumcised Gentiles. So the Jews took steps. At this time the Jewish religion had a special attraction for women. In nothing was the ancient world more soiled and lax than in sexual morality. Family life was rapidly breaking down. The worst sufferers were women. The Jewish religion preached a high austere purity of ethic and cleanness of life. Round the Synagogues there gathered many women, often women of high social position, who found in this teaching just what they so much longed for. Many of these women became proselytes ; still more were God-fearers. The Jews persuaded these women to incite their husbands, who were often magistrates and men in influential positions, to take steps against the Christian preachers. The inevitable result was persecution, and Antioch became unsafe for Paul and Barnabas and they had to go. The Jews were intent on keeping their privileges to themselves. From the beginning the Christians saw that a privilege is granted only to be shared. The Jews were intent on shutting the door. From the beginning the Christians saw that the door must be opened wide.

As it has been said, " The Jews saw the heathen as chaff to be burned ; Jesus saw them as a harvest to be reaped for God." And His Church must have a like vision of a world for Christ.

ON TO ICONIUM

Acts 14 : 1-7

> It happened in Iconium that they went in the same way into the Synagogue of the Jews and spoke to such effect that a great crowd of the Jews and of the Greeks believed. But the Jews who did not believe inflamed the minds of the Gentiles against the brethren. So then, they spent some considerable time boldly speaking in the name of the Lord, who bore witness to the word of His grace by causing signs and wonders to happen through their hands. The population of the city was torn in two. Some sided with the Jews and some with the apostles. When the Gentiles and the Jews with their leaders combined in a movement to assault and stone them, they discovered what was afoot and fled for safety to the cities of Lycaonia, Lystra and Derbe, and the surrounding district. And there they continued to preach the good news.

So Paul and Barnabas went on to Iconium. Iconium was about 90 miles from Antioch. It was an ancient city, so ancient that it claimed to be older than Damascus. In the dim past it had had a king called Nannacus, and the phrase " since the days of Nannacus " was proverbial for " from the beginning of time." As usual they began in the Synagogue and as usual they had good success ; but the jealous Jews stirred up the mob and once again Paul and Barnabas had to move on. It has to be noted that Paul and Barnabas were more and more taking their lives in their hands. What was proposed in Iconium was nothing other than a lynching. The further on Paul and Barnabas went the further they got from civilisation. In the more civilised cities their lives at least were safe because Rome kept order and a lynching would have been speedily punished ; but now, out in the wilds, Paul and Barnabas are to be ever under the threat of mob violence from the excitable Phrygian crowds stirred up by the Jews. Whatever else these two were they were brave men. It always takes courage to be a Christian because it always takes courage to take a way that is different from the crowd.

MISTAKEN FOR GODS AT LYSTRA

Acts 14 : 8-18

There was a man who sat in Lystra who had no power in his feet. He had been a cripple from his birth and he had never walked. He was in the habit of listening to Paul speaking. Paul fixed his gaze on him. He saw that he had faith that he could be cured and he said to him in a loud voice, " Stand up straight on your feet." He leaped up and kept walking about. When the crowds saw what Paul had done they exclaimed in the Lycaonian dialect, " The gods have taken the form of men and have come down to us." They called Barnabas, Zeus ; and Paul, Hermes, because he was the leader in speaking. The priest of Zeus whose shrine is in front of the city brought oxen and wreaths to the gates and he and the crowd wished to offer sacrifice to them. But when the apostles Barnabas and Paul heard this, they rent their clothes and rushed in among the people shouting, " Men, what is this you are doing ? We too are men of like passions with you. We are bringing you the good news which tells you to turn from these empty things to the living God, who made heaven and earth and sea and all that is in them. In past generations He allowed all nations to go their own way. And yet He never left Himself without a witness, for He was kind to men, and He gave you rain from heaven and the fruitful seasons and He filled your hearts with food and gladness." As they said these things they could hardly stop the crowds sacrificing to them.

FROM Iconium, Paul and Barnabas moved on to Lystra and there they were involved in a strange incident. The explanation of their being taken for gods lies in the legendary history of Lycaonia. The people round Lystra told a story that once Zeus and Hermes had come to this earth incognito and in disguise. There was none in all the land who would give them hospitality. At last two old peasants, Philemon and his wife Baucis, took them in and were kind to them. The result was that the whole population was wiped out by the gods except Philemon and Baucis who were made the guardians of a splendid temple and who were turned into two great trees when they died. So when Paul healed the cripple man the people of Lystra were determined this time not to make the same mistake and to ignore the gods again. Barnabas must have been a man of noble presence so they took him for Zeus the king of the gods. Hermes was the god of speech and the messenger of the gods and, since Paul was the speaker, they called him Hermes.

But this passage is specially interesting because it gives us Paul's approach to those who were completely heathen and who had no Jewish background to which he could appeal. When Paul talked to such people he started from nature to get to God. All men knew about the rain and the sun and the seedtime and the harvest ; and Paul started there to lead men's minds to the God who was behind it all. Paul, like the great teacher he was, did what every teacher must do—he started from the here and now to get to the there and then. We would do well sometimes to remember that the world is the garment of the living God. It is told that once, as they sailed in the Mediterranean, Napoleon's suite were discussing God. In the talk they eliminated God altogether. Napoleon had been silent but at the end of the talk he lifted his hand and pointed at the sea and the sky, " Gentlemen," he said, " who made all this ? " Sometimes we would do well to look at the world and remember the God who made all this.

THE COURAGE OF PAUL

Acts 14 : 19, 20

> There came certain Jews from Antioch and Iconium They won over the crowds and they stoned Paul and dragged him outside the city, for they thought he was dead. While the disciples stood in a circle round him he got up and he went into the city ; and on the next day with Barnabas he went away to Derbe.

In the midst of all the excitement at Lystra certain Jews arrived. They may have been there for one of two reasons. They may quite possibly have been deliberately following up Paul and Barnabas in a set attempt to undo the work that they were doing. Or they may have been corn merchants. The region round Lystra was a great corn growing area and they may have come to buy corn for the cities of Iconium and Antioch. If so, they would be shocked and angry to find Paul still preaching and they would very naturally stir up the people against him.

It is true that Lystra was a Roman colony ; but it was an outpost. Nevertheless, when the people saw what they had done they were afraid. That is why they dragged what they thought was Paul's dead body out of the city. They were afraid of the strong hand of Roman justice and they were trying to get rid of Paul's body to escape the consequences of their riot.

But the outstanding feature of this story is the sheer dauntless courage of Paul. When he came to his senses again his first act was to go right back into that city where he had been stoned. It never struck him to run away. It was John Wesley's advice, " Always look a mob in the face." Paul never did a braver thing than to go straight back into the city which had tried to murder him. It is quite clear that a deed like that would have more effect than a hundred sermons. Men were bound to ask themselves whence came the courage that enabled a man to act in such a way.

THE ACTS OF THE APOSTLES

CONFIRMING THE CHURCH

Acts 14 : 21-28

When they had preached the good news to that city and had made a considerable number of disciples they returned to Lystra and to Iconium and to Antioch. As they went they strengthened the souls of the disciples and urged them to abide in the faith, saying, " It is through many an affliction that we must enter into the Kingdom of God." In each Church they chose elders, and, when they had prayed with fasting, they offered them to the Lord in whom they had believed. When they had gone through Pisidia they came to Pamphylia. When they had spoken the word in Perga they went down to Attaleia. From there they sailed away to Antioch, from which they had been handed over to the grace of God for the work which they had completed. On their arrival there, when they had called a meeting of the Church, they told them the story of all that God had done with them and that He had opened the door of faith to the Gentiles. They spent a long time with the disciples.

In this passage there are three notable lights on the mind of Paul. (i) There is his utter honesty to the people who had chosen to become Christians. He frankly told them that it was through many an affliction they would have to enter into the Kingdom of God. He offered them no easy way. He acted on the principle that Jesus had come " not to make life easy but to make men great." (ii) On the return journey Paul set apart elders in all the little groups of newly-made Christians. Paul showed that it was his conviction that from the very beginning Christianity must be lived in a fellowship. People were not left to be isolated individuals living alone. As one of the great fathers put it, " No man can have God for his father unless he has the Church for his mother." As John Wesley put it, " No man ever went to heaven alone ; he must either find friends or make them." From the very beginning it was Paul's aim not only to make individual Christians but to build these individuals into a Christian fellowship (iii) Paul and Barnabas never thought that it was their strength or their power which had achieved anything. They spoke of what God had done with them. They regarded themselves only as fellow-labourers with God. After the great victory of Agincourt, Henry the king forbade any songs or ditties to be made or sung and ordered that all the glory should be given to God. We will begin to have the right idea of Christian service when we work, not for our own honour or prestige, but only from the conviction that we are tools in the hand of God.

THE CRUCIAL PROBLEM

The preaching to the Gentiles and the influx of the Gentiles into the Church produced a problem which had to be solved. The whole mental background of the Jew was founded on the fact that he belonged to the chosen people. In reality and in effect they believed that not only were the Jews the peculiar possession of God but also that God was the peculiar possession of the Jews. The problem was this. Before a Gentile became a Christian and a member of the Christian Church was it necessary that he should be circumcised and take upon himself the Law of Moses ? In other words—Must the Gentile, before he became a Christian, first become a Jew ? Or, could a Gentile be received into the Church as such ? Was he eligible for acceptance simply as a man ? But even were that question settled there arose another problem. The strict Jew could have no intercourse with a Gentile. He could not have him as guest nor yet be his guest. He would not, as far as possible, even do business with him. So then there arose the question—Even if the Gentiles are allowed into the Church, in how far can Jews and Gentiles associate in the ordinary social life of the Church and of the world ? If the Gentiles are allowed in are the lines of demarcation to continue even in the Church ?

Or, were Gentiles and Jews to be on the same footing with no difference at all ? These were the problems which had to be solved. The solution was not easy. But in the end the Church took the decision that there should be no difference between Jew and Gentile at all. It is the 15th chapter of Acts which tells of the Council of Jerusalem which took that decision. Its decisions were the charter of freedom for the Gentiles.

A PROBLEM BECOMES ACUTE

Acts 15 : 1-5

> Some men came down from Judaea and tried to teach the brethren, " If you are not circumcised according to the practice of Moses you cannot be saved." When Paul and Barnabas had a great dispute and argument with them, they arranged for Paul and Barnabas and some others of them to go up to Jerusalem to the apostles and elders to get this question settled. So they were sent on their way by the Church, and they passed through Phoenicia and Samaria telling the story of the conversion of the Gentiles ; and they brought great joy to all the brethren. When they arrived at Jerusalem they were received by the Church and the apostles and the elders and they told the story of all that God had done with them. But some men of the school of the Pharisees, who were converts, rose and said, " It is necessary to circumcise them and to enjoin them to keep the Law of Moses."

IT was almost by accident that the most epoch-making things had happened and were happening in Antioch. The gospel was being preached to Jew and to Gentile alike and Jew and Gentile were living together as brethren. Now there were certain Jews to whom all this was quite unthinkable. They could never forget the position of the Jews as the chosen people. They were quite willing that the Gentiles should come into the Church on the condition that first they became Jews and accepted the Law, in fact on condition that first they became Jews. If this attitude had prevailed inevitably Christianity would have become nothing other than a sect of Judaism. Some of these narrower Jews came down to Antioch and tried to persuade the converts that they would lose everything unless they first accept Judaism. Very naturally Paul and Barnabas argued strongly against this. Matters came to a deadlock. There was only one way out. An appeal must be made to Jerusalem, to the headquarters of the Church and a final decision one way or another must be taken. The case which Paul and Barnabas put forward was simply the story of what had happened. They were prepared to let the facts speak for themselves. There were certain of the Pharisees who had become Christians. The very name Pharisee means the separated one. They had separated themselves from all men in one life-long attempt to keep the last detail of the Law. They insisted that all converts must be circumcised and must keep the Law. The argument was on in all its sharp division.

The principle at stake was quite simple and completely fundamental. It was—Is the gift of God for the select few or for all the world? If we possess it ourselves are we to look on it as a privilege specially given to us, or as a responsibility laid upon us? The problem may not meet us nowadays in precisely the same way; but the fact remains that there still exist divisions between class and class, between nation and nation, between colour and colour. We only fully realize the true meaning of Christianity when all middle walls of partition are broken down.

PETER STATES THE CASE

Acts 15 : 6-12

The apostles and elders met together to investigate this question. After a great deal of discussion Peter stood up and said, " Brethren, you know that in the early days God made His choice among us, so that through my mouth the Gentiles should hear the good news and believe. And God, who knows men's hearts, bore His own witness to them by giving them the Holy Spirit just as He had done to us too. He made no distinction between us and them for He purified their hearts by faith. So why do you now tempt God by placing on the necks of the disciples a yoke which neither our fathers nor we had the strength to bear ? But it is through the grace of Jesus Christ that we believe that we have been saved in exactly the same way as they too have been." The whole assembly was silent and listened to Barnabas and Paul as they told the story of all the signs and wonders God had done amongst the heathen through them.

In answer to the Pharisees and the stricter Jews, Peter reminded them of how he himself had been responsible for the reception of Cornelius into the Church in the early days, ten years before this. The proof that he had acted rightly was that God had granted His Holy Spirit to these very Gentiles who had been received. As far as the Law's claims went they might have been ceremonially unclean ; but God had done a far greater thing—by His Spirit He had cleansed their hearts. Peter demanded, " What man had ever found happiness through the Law ? " The attempt to obey its multifarious commands and to earn salvation was a losing battle which left every man in default. There is only one way for every man—the acceptance of the free gift of the grace of God in an act of self-surrendering and humble faith.

Peter went right to the heart of the question. In this whole debate and dispute the deepest of deep principles was involved. It was this. Can a man earn the favour of God ? Can he justify himself by his own efforts ? Can he himself by obedience to the Law make himself right with God ? Or, must he admit his own helplessness and powerlessness and be ready in humble faith to accept what the grace of God gives and what he himself could never earn ? In effect, the Jewish party said, " Religion means earning God's favour by keeping the Law." In effect Peter said, " Religion consists in casting ourselves on the grace and the love of God." Here there is implicit the difference between a religion of works and a religion of grace. Peace will never come to any man until he realizes that he can never put God in his debt ; but that he can only take what God in His grace gives. The paradox of Christianity is that the way to victory is the way of surrender ; and the way to power is to admit one's own helplessness.

THE LEADERSHIP OF JAMES

Acts 15 : 13-21

> After they had been silent James replied, "Brothers, listen to me. Symeon has told you how God first made provision for the Gentiles, to take from them a people for His name. With this the words of the prophets agree, as it stands written, ' After these things I will return and I will build again the tabernacle of David which has fallen. I will build its ruins again, and again I will set it upright, so that the rest of mankind will seek the Lord, even all the Gentiles who are called by My name'—this is what the Lord says, making these things known from the beginning of the world. Therefore, for my part, it is my judgment that we stop making things difficult for the Gentiles who turn to God, but that we send them a letter to keep themselves from the contaminations offered to idols, from fornication, from things strangled and from blood. For Moses from of old has those who proclaim his teaching in every city, for his works are read in the Synagogues every Sabbath."

WE may well believe that the matter of the reception of the Gentiles hung in the balance ; and then James spoke. The position of James was all important. He was the leader of the Jerusalem Church. His leadership was not that of an official office ; it was a moral leadership conceded to him because he was an outstanding man. He was the brother of Jesus Himself. He had had a special resurrection appearance of Jesus all to himself (I Corinthians 15 : 7). He was a pillar of the Church (Galatians I : 19). He was so constant in prayer that his knees were said to be as hard as a camel's because he knelt so often and so long. He was so good a man that he was called James the Just. And further—and this was all-important—he himself was a rigorous observer of the Law. If this man the pillar and the crown of orthodoxy came down on the side of the Gentiles then all was well. And James did. It was his judgment that the disciples should be allowed into the Church without let or hindrance. But even when they were allowed in, the matter of ordinary social intercourse came in. How could a strict and orthodox Jew consort with a Gentile ? To make things easier James suggested certain regulations that Gentiles must keep. They must abstain from the contaminations of idols. That was a food regulation. One of the great problems of the early Church was the problem of meat offered to idols. Paul deals with it at length in I Corinthians 8 and 9. What was behind this ? When a heathen sacrificed in a temple, often only a very small part of the meat was sacrificed. The rest was given back to him to make a feast for his friends, often in the temple precincts, sometimes in his own house. When meat was sacrificed the priests received part of it and that part was then sold for ordinary purposes. Such meat had been offered to an idol and the idols were really demons and devils. No Christian must risk pollution by eating such meat. They must abstain from fornication. It has been said that chastity was the only completely new virtue that Christianity brought into the world. The Christian must be pure in an impure world. They must abstain from things strangled and from blood. To the Jew the blood was the life. They so argued because when the blood flowed away life ebbed away too. Therefore all Jewish meat was killed and treated in such a way that the blood was drained off, for the blood was the life and the life belonged to God. So the Gentile is ordered to eat only meat prepared in the Jewish way. Had these simple regulations not been observed there could have been no intercourse between Jew and Gentile ; but the observation of these simple rules destroyed the last barrier. Within the Church and within the human fellowship from this time the principle was established that Jew and Gentile were one.

THE DECREE GOES OUT

Acts 15 : 22-35

Then the apostles and the elders together with the whole Church took a decision, to choose men from their number and to send them to Antioch with Paul and Barnabas. They chose Judas who is called Barsabas and Silas, men who were leaders among the brethren, and they sent a written message by their hand. " The apostles and the elders, brethren, to the brethren from the Gentiles who are throughout Antioch and Syria and Cilicia—greetings. We have heard that some who came from us have disturbed you with their words in an attempt to upset your souls. They were not acting under our instructions. We have therefore decided, when we were met together, to choose men and to send them to you, with our beloved Barnabas and Paul, who are men who have devoted their lives for the name of the Lord Jesus Christ. We have therefore despatched Judas and Silas to you to tell you the same things by word of mouth. It was the decision of the Holy Spirit and of us to place no further burden on you other than the rules which are necessary—that you should keep yourselves from things offered to idols, from blood, from things strangled and from fornication. If you keep yourselves from these things you will be doing well. Farewell." So these were sent away and came down to Antioch. They called the congregation together and delivered the letter to them. When they had read it they rejoiced at the message of comfort. Judas and Silas, who were themselves prophets, exhorted the brethren with many an address and strengthened them. After spending some time there they were sent away with every good wish for their welfare from the brethren to those who had sent them. But Paul and Barnabas with certain others too stayed in Antioch teaching and telling the good news of the word of the Lord.

ONCE the Church had come to its decision it acted with both efficiency and courtesy. The terms of the decision were embodied in a letter. But the letter was sent by no common messenger ; it was entrusted to Judas and to Silas who went to Antioch with Paul and Barnabas. Had Paul and Barnabas come back alone their enemies might have doubted that they really did bring back a correct message ; but Judas and Silas were official emissaries and guarantors of the reality of the decision. The Church was wise in sending a person as well as a letter. One of the earliest Christian writers declared that he had learned more from the living and the abiding voice than from any amount of reading. A letter could have sounded coldly official ; but the warm words and the wise teaching of Judas and Silas added a friendly warmth that the bare reception of a letter could never have achieved. It is a simple and a practical thing always to remember what trouble has arisen when a letter has been sent which would never have arisen had a personal visit been paid. The Church not only took a wise decision but took the wisest means of putting that decision into effective action.

PAUL TAKES THE ROAD AGAIN

Acts 15 : 36-41

Some time after, Paul said to Barnabas, " Come now, let us go back and visit the brethren in every city in which we preached the word of the Lord, so that we may see how things are going with them." Barnabas wished to take John who was called Mark along with them ; but Paul did not think it right to take with them one who had deserted them in Pamphylia and had not gone with them to the work. There was so sharp a difference of opinion that they were separated from each other and Barnabas took Mark with him and sailed away to Cyprus ; but Paul chose Silas and went off when he had been commended by the brethren to the grace of the Lord. He went through Syria and Cilicia strengthening the Churches.

PAUL was a born adventurer and he could never stay long in the one place. So he decided to take the road again ; but the preparations for the journey ended in a tragic breach. Barnabas wished to take John Mark with them again but Paul would have nothing to do with the man who had played the deserter in Pamphylia. The difference between them was so sharp that they split company never to work with each other again. It is impossible to say whether Barnabas or Paul was right. But this much is true, Mark was supremely fortunate that he had a friend like Barnabas. We have already seen that in the end Mark became the man who redeemed himself. It may well have been the friendship of Barnabas, the man of the kindly heart, which gave Mark back his self-respect and which made him determined to make good. The greatest thing that a man can have is someone who believes in him. Barnabas believed in Mark and in the end Mark justified that belief.

THE SECOND MISSIONARY JOURNEY

The narrative of Paul's second missionary journey, which occupied him for about three years is given us in the section of Acts which extends from 15 : 36 to 18 : 23. It began from Antioch. Paul first made a tour of the Churches of Syria and Cilicia. Then he re-visited the Churches in the regions of Derbe, Lystra, Iconium and Pisidian Antioch. There followed a period when he could not see his way clear before him. That time of uncertainty ended with the vision at Troas. From Troas, Paul crossed to Neapolis and thence to Philippi. From Philippi he moved on to Thessalonica and Beroea. From there he went to Athens and then on to Corinth where he spent about eighteen months. From Corinth he travelled to Jerusalem by way of Ephesus and so finally back to Antioch, his starting point. The great step forward is that with this journey Paul's activity passed beyond Asia Minor and entered Europe.

A SON IN THE FAITH

Acts 16 : 1-5

> Paul arrived at Derbe and Lystra, and, look you, there was a disciple there called Timothy. He was the son of a Jewish woman who was a believer but his father was Greek. The brethren in Lystra and Iconium were witnesses to his worth. Paul wished him to go out with him and he took him and circumcised him because of the Jews who were in these places, for they all knew that his father was Greek. As they made their way through the cities they handed over to them the decisions which had been arrived at by the apostles and elders in Jerusalem, that they should observe them. The Churches were strengthened in the faith and increased in number every day.

IT was five years since Paul had preached in Derbe and Lystra but when he returned his heart must have been gladdened for there had emerged there a young man who was to be very dear to Paul. It was only natural that Paul should be looking for someone to take Mark's place. He was always well aware of the necessity of training a new generation for the work and for the days that lay ahead. He found just the kind of man he wanted in young Timothy. On the face of it, it is something of a problem why Paul circumcised Timothy. He had just won a battle in which circumcision had been declared unnecessary. The reason was that Timothy was a Jew and Paul had never said that circumcision was not necessary for Jews.

It was the Gentiles who were freed from the ceremonies of the Jewish way of life. In point of fact by accepting Timothy as a Jew, Paul showed just how emancipated he was from Jewish thought. Timothy was the son of a mixed marriage. The strict Jew would have refused to accept that as a marriage at all. In the case of a really strict Jew, if a Jewish girl married a Gentile boy, or a Jewish boy married a Gentile girl, that Jewish boy or girl was regarded as dead. So much so, that sometimes their funeral was actually carried out. By accepting the child of such a marriage as a brother Jew, Paul showed how definitely he had broken down all national barriers. Timothy was a lad with a great heritage. He had had a good mother and a good grandmother (2 Timothy 1 : 5). Often in the days to come he was to be Paul's messenger (I Corinthians 4 : 17 ; I Thessalonians 3 : 2-6). He was at Rome with Paul when Paul was in prison (Philippians 1 : 1 ; 2 : 19; Colossians 1 : 1; Philemon 1). Timothy was in a very special relationship to Paul. When Paul wrote to the Corinthians (I Corinthians 4 : 17) he called him his beloved son. When he wrote to the Philippians he said that there was no one whose mind was so much at one with his own (Philippians 2 : 19). It seems very likely that Paul saw in Timothy his own successor when he had to lay down his work. Happy indeed is the man to whom it is given to see the result of his training and teaching in one who can take up the burden when he lays it down.

THE GOSPEL COMES TO EUROPE

Acts 16 : 6-10

They went through the Phrygian and Galatian territory, but they were prevented by the Holy Spirit from speaking the word in Asia. When they had gone through Mysia they tried to go into Bithynia ; and the Spirit of Jesus did not allow them to do so. So they passed by Mysia and came down to Troas.

> During the night a vision appeared to Paul. A man from Macedonia stood and urged him, "Cross over into Macedonia and help us." When he saw the vision he immediately sought to go forth into Macedonia for we reckoned that God had called us to tell the good news to them.

FOR a time all doors seemed shut to Paul. It must have seemed strange to him that he was barred from the Roman province of Asia by the Holy Spirit. Therein lay Ephesus and all the other seven cities whose churches received the letters to the seven Churches in the Book of the Revelation. Bithynia too was shut to him. How did the Holy Spirit send His message to Paul? It may have been by the word of some prophet; it may have been by some vision; it may have been by some inner and inescapable and unmistakable conviction. But there is at least the possibility that what kept Paul from journeying into these provinces was ill-health, the consequence of that thorn in his flesh. What makes that quite likely is that in verse 10 there quite suddenly and without warning emerges a "we" passage. The story begins to be told not in the third person but in the first person. That tells us that Luke was there, an eye-witness and a companion of Paul. Why then should Luke so suddenly emerge on to the scene? What was Luke? Luke was a doctor. What is more likely than that Luke met Paul then because Paul needed his professional services, because he was in ill-health which barred him from making the journeys he would like? If this is so it is a great thought to think that Paul took even his weakness and his pain as a messenger from God. It was the sight of a man from Macedonia which finally gave Paul his guidance where to go. Who was this man Paul saw in the vision? Some think it was Luke himself, for Luke may have been a Macedonian. Some think the question should not be asked for dreams need no explanations like that. But there is one most attractive theory. There was one man who had succeeded in conquering the world. That was Alexander the Great. Now it would seem that the whole situation was designed to make Paul remember Alexander. The full name of Troas was Alexandrian Troas ; it was called after Alexander. Just across the sea was Philippi called after Alexander's father. Just farther on there was Thessalonica called after Alexander's half-sister. The district was permeated with memories of Alexander ; and Alexander was the man who had said that his aim was " to marry the east to the west," and so to make one world. It may well be that at this moment, as Paul meditated his step from east to west, from Asia Minor to Europe, there came to him the vision of Alexander, the man who had conquered a world, and that that vision gave to Paul a new impulse towards making one world for Christ.

EUROPE'S FIRST CONVERT

Acts 16 : 11-15

> When we had set sail from Troas we had a straight run to Samothrace. On the next day we reached Neapolis and from there we came to Philippi which is the chief city of that section of Macedonia and a Roman colony. We spent some days in this city. On the Sabbath day we went outside the gates along the riverside where we believed there was a place of prayer. We sat down and were talking with the women who met together there. A woman whose name was Lydia, who was a purple seller from the city of Thyatira, who reverenced God, listened to us. God opened her heart so that she gave heed to the things said by Paul. When she and her household had been baptized she urged us, " If you judge me to be faithful to the Lord, come into my house and stay there." And she pressed us to do so.

NEAPOLIS—the modern Kavalla—was the seaport of Philippi. Philippi had a long history. Once it had been called Crenides which means " The Springs." But Philip of Macedon, the father of Alexander, had fortified it as a barrier against the Thracians and had given it his own name. At one time it had possessed famous gold mines, but by Paul's time, these mines were worked out. Later it had been the scene of one of the most famous battles in the world, when Augustus won for himself the Roman Empire. It was a Roman colony. That is to say it was a little bit of Rome planted in a foreign land. Roman colonies were usually strategic centres. In them Rome planted little groups of army veterans who had completed their military service. These colonists wore the Roman dress, spoke the Roman language and used the Roman laws no matter where they were. Nowhere was there greater pride in Roman citizenship than in these outposts of Rome. In Philippi there was no Synagogue from which to start. But where the Jews were unable to have a Synagogue they had a place of prayer and these places of prayer were usually by the riverside. Thither on the Sabbath Paul and his friends took their way and there they talked with the women who met there. Now the extraordinary thing about Paul's work in Philippi is the amazing cross-section of the population that was won for Christ. This section tells us of Lydia and she came from the very top end of the social scale. She was a purple merchant. The purple dye had to be gathered drop by drop from a certain shell-fish. It was so costly that a pound of wool dyed with it could cost as much as £40. Lydia was a wealthy woman and a merchant prince. She was won for Christ. And we must note her immediate reaction—she immediately offered the hospitality of her house to Paul and his friends. When Paul is describing the Christian character he says that the Christian should be " given to hospitality " (Romans 12 : 13). When Peter is urging the Christian duty upon his converts he tells them, " Use hospitality to each other and never grudge it " (I Peter 4 : 9). A Christian home is a home with an ever-open door.

THE DEMENTED SLAVE-GIRL

Acts 16 : 16-24

When we were on our way to the place of prayer, it happened that a certain slave-girl who had a spirit which made her able to give oracles met us. By her soothsaying she provided much gain for her owners. As she followed Paul and us she kept shouting, " These men are the slaves of the most high God and they are proclaiming the way of salvation to you." She kept doing this for many days. Paul was vexed at this and he turned and said to the spirit, " In the name of Jesus Christ I order you to come out of her." And it came out that very hour.

When her owners saw that their hope of gain was gone they laid hands on Paul and Silas and dragged them to the city square to the magistrates. So they brought them to the chief magistrates and said, " These men, who are Jews, are disturbing the whole city and are proclaiming customs which it is not right for us who are Romans to receive." The crowd came together against them. The chief magistrates tore off their clothes and ordered them to be scourged with rods. When they had laid many blows upon them they threw them into prison with instructions to the gaoler to guard them securely. When he received such an order he flung them into the inner prison and secured their feet in the stocks.

WE have already said that the converts Paul made and the people with whom he came into contact in Philippi present a most amazing cross-section of the population. If Lydia came from the top end of the social scale this slave-girl came from the bottom. She was what was called a Pytho and a Pytho was a person who could give oracles to guide men about the future. She was mad and the ancient world had a queer respect for mad people for, they said, the gods had taken away their wits to put the mind of the gods into them. She was probably also gifted with a natural turn for ventriloquism. She had fallen into the hands of unscrupulous men who used her misfortune for their great gain. When Paul cured her of her madness the one thing that these men felt was not joy at a fellow creature's restoration to health and sanity but fury that their source of revenue was gone. They were astute men. They played on the natural anti-semitism of the mob ; and they appealed to the pride in things Roman which was characteristic of a Roman colony and they succeeded in having Paul and Silas arrested. Not only were they arrested ; they were put in the inner prison in the stocks. It may be that not only their feet, but their hands and their necks also were held in the stocks. The tragic thing is that Paul and Silas were arrested and maltreated for doing good. Whenever Christianity attacks vested interest trouble follows. It is characteristic of men that if their pockets are touched and their profits are threatened they are up in arms. It is every man's duty to ask himself, " Is the money I am earning worth the price ? Do I earn it by serving or by exploiting my fellow men ? " Often, if not always, the greatest obstacle to the crusade of Christ is the selfishness of men.

THE PHILIPPIAN GAOLER

Acts 16 : 25-40

About midnight Paul and Silas were praying and singing hymns to God, and the prisoners were listening to them. Suddenly there was a great earthquake so that the foundations of the prison were shaken. Immediately the doors were opened and everyone's bonds were loosed. When the gaoler woke up and saw the doors of the prison standing open he drew his sword and he was going to kill himself for he thought that the prisoners had escaped. But Paul shouted to him, " Do yourself no harm for we are all here." He called for a light and rushed in. He fell in terror before Paul and Silas and brought them out and said, " Sirs, what must I do to be saved ? " They said, " Believe on the Lord Jesus and you and your house will be saved." And they spoke the Lord's word to him together with all in his house. And that very hour he took them and washed their weals and he and his household were immediately baptized. He brought them into his house and set a meal before them and he rejoiced with all his house when he had believed in God.

When day came the chief magistrates sent their officers saying, " Let these men go." The gaoler brought the message to Paul, " The chief magistrates have sent word that you are to be released. So now, go out and go your way in peace." But Paul said to them, " They beat us and they put us into prison although we never had a trial—and we are Romans. And now are they going to put us out secretly ? Certainly not ! Let them come themselves and bring us out." The officers told the chief magistrates what Paul had said. They were afraid when they heard that they were Romans. So they came and requested them and brought them out and asked them to leave the city. When they had come out of prison they visited Lydia. They saw the brethren and exhorted them and went away.

If Lydia came from the top end of the social scale and the slave girl from the bottom, the Roman gaoler was one of the sturdy middle class who made up the Roman civil service ; and so in these three the whole gamut of society was complete. Let us look first of all at the *scene* of this passage. This was a district where earthquakes were by no means uncommon. The door was locked by a wooden bar falling into two slots and the stocks were similarly fastened. The earthquake shook the bar free and the prisoners were unfettered and the door was open. The gaoler was about to kill himself because Roman law said that if a prisoner escaped the gaoler must suffer the penalty the prisoner would have suffered. Now let us look at the *characters*. First, there is Paul. We note three things about Paul. (i) He could sing hymns when he was fast in the stocks in the inner prison at midnight. The one thing you can never take away from a Christian is God and the presence of Jesus Christ. With God there is freedom even in a prison and even at midnight there is light. (ii) He was quite willing to open the door of salvation to the gaoler who had shut the door of the prison on him. There was never a grudge in Paul's nature. He would preach to the very man who had fastened him in the stocks. (iii) He could stand on his dignity. He claimed his rights as a Roman citizen. To scourge a Roman citizen was a crime punishable by death. But Paul was not standing on his dignity for his own sake but for the sake of the Christians he was leaving behind in Philippi. He wanted it to be seen that they were not without influential friends. Second of the characters there is the gaoler. The interesting thing about the gaoler is that he immediately confirmed and proved his conversion by his deeds. No sooner had he turned to Christ than he washed the weals upon the prisoners' backs and set a meal before them. His Christianity issued there and then in the most practical act of kindness. Unless a man's Christianity makes him kind it is not Christianity at all. Unless a man's change of heart is guaranteed by his change of deeds it is a spurious and a counterfeit thing.

IN THESSALONICA

Acts 17 : 1-9

When they had taken the road through Amphipolis and Apollonia, they came to Thessalonica where there was a Synagogue of the Jews. Paul, as his custom was, went in to them and, for three Sabbaths, he debated with them from the scriptures, opening the scriptures to them and presenting the evidence that Christ had to suffer and to rise from the dead, " and this man," he said, " is the Christ, Jesus whom I proclaim to you." Some of them believed and threw in their lot with Paul and Silas. Thus it was with many of the worshipping Greeks and with a considerable number of women who belonged to the most influential ranks of society. The Jews resented this. They got hold of some of the low characters who haunted the market place and they formed a mob and set the city in an uproar. They surged up to Jason's house and kept demanding that they should bring them before the people. When they did not find them, they dragged Jason and some of the brethren to the city magistrates, shouting, " These men who have upset the civilised world have arrived here too ; and Jason has received them as his guests. These are all teaching against the decrees of Caesar for they say that there is another emperor—Jesus." They disturbed the mob and the chief magistrates as they heard this. So they took surety from Jason and the others and let them go.

THE coming of Christianity to Thessalonica was an event of the first importance. The great Roman road from the Adriatic Sea to the Middle East was called the Egnatian Way; and the main street of Thessalonica was actually part of that road. If Christianity was firmly founded in Thessalonica it could spread both east and west along that road until the road become a very highway of the progress of the Kingdom of God. The first verse of this chapter is an extraordinary example of the economy of the writer of Acts. It sounds like a pleasant stroll ; but in point of fact Philippi was 33 Roman miles from Amphipolis ; Amphipolis was 30 miles from Apollonia ; and Apollonia was 37 miles from Thessalonica. A journey of over 100 miles is dismissed in a sentence. As usual Paul began his work in Thessalonica in the Synagogue. His great success was not so much among the Jews as among the Gentiles who were attached to the Synagogue because of the attraction of the Jewish faith. This infuriated the Jews for they looked on these very Gentiles as their natural preserves and Paul was stealing them. as they thought, before their very eyes. The methods the Jews took to stop Paul were low in the extreme. In the days of the French Revolution, Madame Roland uttered the famous sentence, " Liberty, what crimes are committed in thy name." The Jews stooped to the lowest methods to hinder Paul. First they aroused people who could only be described as " the corner boys of Thessalonica." Then when they had dragged Jason and his friends before the magistrates they charged the Christian preachers with preaching political insurrection and rebellion—a charge which they knew was a lie. And yet the charge is an intensely suggestive one. " Those," they said, " who are upsetting the civilised world have arrived here." That is one of the greatest compliments which has ever been paid to Christianity. The Jews had not the slightest doubt that Christianity was a supremely *effective* thing. Further, it is a challenge. T. R. Glover quoted with delight the saying of the child who remarked that the New Testament ended with *Revolutions*. When Christianity really goes into action it must cause a revolution both in the life of the individual and in the life of society.

ON TO BEROEA

Acts 17 : 10-15

> The brethren immediately sent Paul and Silas away to Beroea by night. When they arrived there they came into the Synagogue of the Jews. These were men of finer character than those in Thessalonica, and they received the word with all eagerness. They daily examined the scriptures to see if these things were so. Many of them believed, as did a considerable number of well-to-do Greek women and men. When the Jews of Thessalonica knew that the word of God was preached by Paul in Beroea they came there too in an attempt to stir up and disturb the people. The brethren then immediately sent Paul away as far as the sea coast, while Silas and Timothy remained there. Those who conducted Paul brought him as far as Athens ; and when they had received an order to tell Silas and Timothy to come to him with all speed, they went away.

BEROEA was 60 miles west of Thessalonica. Three things stand out in this short section. (i) The preaching of Paul was almost entirely scriptural. He set the people of Beroea searching the scriptures. The one thing that made the Jews certain that Jesus was not the Messiah was the fact that He had been crucified. To them a man who had been crucified was a man accursed. It was no doubt in passages like Isaiah 53 that Paul set the people of Beroea to find a forecast of the work of Jesus. (ii) There stands out the envenomed bitterness of Jews. They not only opposed Paul in Thessalonica ; they pursued him to Beroea. The tragedy is that undoubtedly they thought that they were doing God's work by seeking to silence Paul. It can be a terrible thing when a man identifies his aims with the will of God instead of submitting his ways to that will. (iii) There stands out once again the courage of Paul. He had been imprisoned in Philippi. He had left Thessalonica in peril of his life and under cover of darkness. And once again in Beroea he had to flee for his life. Most men would have abandoned a struggle which seemed bound to end in arrest and in death. When David Livingstone was asked where he was prepared to go, he answered, " I am prepared to go anywhere, *so long as it is forward.*" The idea of turning back never occurred to Paul.

ALONE IN ATHENS

Acts 17 : 16-21

When Paul was waiting for them in Athens his spirit was deeply vexed as he saw the whole city full of idols. He debated with the Jews and the worshippers in the Synagogue and every day he talked in the city square with everyone he met. Some of the Epicurean and Stoic philosophers took issue with him. Some of them said, " What would this gutter-sparrow of a man be saying ? " Others said, " He seems to be the herald of strange divinities." This they said because he told the good news of Jesus and the Resurrection. So they took him and brought him to the Areopagus saying, " May we know what this strange new teaching you are talking about is ? For you are introducing things which sound strange to us. We want therefore to know what these things mean." (All the Athenians and the strangers who stay there have no time for anything other than to talk about and to listen to the latest idea).

WHEN he fled from Beroea, Paul found himself alone in Athens. But with comrades or alone Paul never stopped preaching Christ. Athens had long since left behind her great days of action but she was still the greatest university town in the world, to which men seeking learning came from all over the world. She was a city of many gods. It was said that there were more statues of the gods in Athens than in all the rest of Greece put together, and that in Athens it was easier to meet a god than a man. In the great city square people met to talk, for in Athens they did little else. The days of action were past and now men talked all day and half the night about the newest idea. So Paul would have no difficulty in getting someone to talk to. The philosophers discovered him. There were the Epicureans. We may sum up their beliefs in this way. (i) They believed that everything happened by chance. (ii) They believed that death was the end of all. (iii) They believed that there were gods but the gods were remote from the world and did not care. (iv) They believed that pleasure was the chief end of man. They did not mean fleshly and worldly and material pleasure ; for the highest pleasure was the pleasure that brought no pain to follow. There were the Stoics. We may sum up their beliefs in this way. (i) They believed that literally everything was God. God was fiery spirit. That spirit grew blunt and dull in matter but it was in everything. What gave men life was that a little spark of that spirit dwelt in them and when they died it returned to God. But for the Stoic everything was God. (ii) They believed that everything was fated because everything was the will of God ; and therefore whatever happened we must not care. It is God's will and must be accepted. (iii) They believed that every so many years the world disintegrated in a conflagration and then started all over again on the same story. They took Paul to the Areopagus which is the Greek for Mars' Hill. It was the name both of the hill and the court that met on it. The court was very select, only perhaps thirty members. It dealt with cases of homicide and had the oversight of public morals. So in the most learned city in the world, before the most exclusive of courts, Paul had to state his faith. It might have daunted anyone ; but Paul was never ashamed of the gospel of Christ. To him it was only another God-given opportunity to witness for Christ.

A SERMON TO THE PHILOSOPHERS

Acts 17 : 22-31

Paul stood up in the midst of the Aeropagus and said, " Men of Athens, I see that in all things you are as superstitious as possible. As I came through your city and as I saw the objects of your worship, I found amongst them an altar with the inscription, ' To the Unknown God.' So then, what you worship and do not know, this I preach to you. God, who made the universe and everything in it, this God is Lord of heaven and earth and does not dwell in temples made with hands ; nor is He served by the hands of men, as if He needed anything, but He Himself gives to all life and breath and all things. He made of one every race of men to dwell on all the face of the earth, and He fixed the appointed times and boundaries of their habitations. He made men so that they might search for God, if they might perchance feel after Him and find Him ; and indeed He is not far from any one of us. For by Him we live and move and are. As some of your own poets have said, ' We too are His offspring.' Since then we are the offspring of God we should not think that the Divine is like gold or silver or stone, engraved by the art and design of man. So then God overlooked the times of ignorance but now He gives orders to men that all men everywhere should repent. Thus He has fixed a day in which He will judge the world in righteousness by a man whom He ordained for that task, and He has given proof of this by raising Him from the dead."

THERE were in fact many altars to unknown gods in Athens. Six hundred years before this a terrible pestilence had fallen on the city. Nothing could halt it. A Cretan poet, Epimenides, had come forward with a plan. A flock of black and white sheep were let loose throughout the city from the Areopagus. Wherever each lay down it was sacrificed to the nearest god ; and if a sheep lay down near the shrine of no known god it was sacrificed to " The Unknown God." Athens had its regiment of unknown gods. From that Paul takes his starting point. Paul could fit his message for any audience. There are a series of steps in his sermon. (i) God is not the made but the maker, therefore He who made all things cannot be worshipped by anything made by the hands of man. It is all too true that men often worship what their hands have made. If a man's God be that to which he gives all his time, thought, energy, life, many a man is engaged in worshipping material, man-made things. (ii) God has guided history. It was He who had been behind the rise and fall of nations in the days gone by. His hand was and is on the helm of things. (iii) God has made man so that instinctively he longs for God. There is that in man which makes him grope in the darkness after God because man is a child of God and kin to God. (iv) The days of groping and ignorance are past. So long as men had to search in the shadows they could not know God and God excused their follies and their mistakes ; but now in Christ the full blaze of the knowledge and revelation of God have come. The days of excuses are past because now the truth has come. (v) The day of judgment is coming For man life is neither a progress to extinction, as it was to the Epicureans, nor yet a pathway to absorption to God, as it was to the Stoics ; it was a journey to the judgment seat of God where Jesus Christ was Judge. (vi) The proof of the pre-eminence of Christ is the Resurrection. It is no unknown God but a Risen Christ with whom we have to deal.

THE REACTIONS OF THE ATHENIANS

Acts 17 : 32-34

> When they heard of a resurrection of dead men, some mocked, and some said, "We will hear about this again"; but some attached themselves to him and believed. Amongst these were Dionysius the Areopagite and a woman called Damaris, together with others.

It would seem on the whole that Paul had less success in Athens than anywhere else. It was typical of the Athenians that all they wanted was to talk. They did not want action; they did not even particularly want conclusions. All they wanted was mental acrobatics and the stimulus of a mental hike. They were lost in words. There were three main reactions. (i) Some mocked. They were amused by the passionate earnestness of this strange Jew. It is possible to make a jest of life; but those who make a jest of life will find that that which began as comedy must end in tragedy. (ii) Some said, "We will hear about this again." Some, that is to say, put off their decision. The most dangerous of all days is when a man discovers how easy it is to talk about to-morrow. (iii) Some believed. Some accepted the terms of God. The wise man knows that only the fool will reject the offer of God.

Here again we may well have an example of the universal appeal of the gospel. Two converts are named. There is Dionysius the Areopagite. We have already said that that court was composed of perhaps not more than thirty people. Dionysius must have been one of the intellectual aristocracy of Athens. There was Damaris. The position of women in Athens was very restricted. It is far from likely that any respectable woman would have been in the market square at all. The likelihood is that she turned from a way of shame to a way of life. Once again the gospel made its appeal to all classes and conditions of men and women.

144

PREACHING IN CORINTH

Its very position made Corinth a key city of Greece. Greece is almost cut in two by the sea. On the one side there is the Saronic Gulf with its port of Cenchrea and on the other there is the Corinthian Gulf with its port of Lechaeum. Between the two there was a neck of land less than five miles across and on that isthmus stood Corinth. The result was that all north and south traffic in Greece had to pass through Corinth because there was no other way. Men called her " The Bridge of Greece." But the voyage round the southern extremity of Greece was a voyage of great peril. The southernmost cape was Cape Malea and to round Cape Malea was the equivalent of rounding Cape Horn. The Greeks had a proverb, " Let him who thinks of sailing round Malea make his will." Consequently the east to west trade of the Mediterranean also passed through Corinth, for men chose that way rather than the perilous voyage round Malea. Corinth was " the market place of Greece."

But Corinth was more than a great commercial centre. She was the home of the Isthmian Games which were second only to the Olympic Games. But above all she was a wicked city. The Greeks had a verb, " to play the Corinthian," which meant to life a life of lustful debauchery. The word " Corinthian " came into the English language to describe in regency times a reckless, roystering regency buck. In Greece if ever a Corinthian was shown on the stage he was shown drunk. Dominating Corinth there stood the hill of the Acropolis. The hill was not only a fortress ; it was a temple of Aphrodite. In its great days the temple had one thousand priestesses of Aphrodite who were sacred prostitutes and who, at evening, came down to the city streets to ply their trade. It had become a proverb, " Not every man can afford a journey to Corinth." It was in a city like that that Paul lived and worked and had some of his greatest triumphs. When he was writing to the Corinthians he made a list of all kinds of wickedness. " Know ye not that the unrighteous shall not inherit the kingdom of God ? Be not deceived : neither fornicators, nor idolaters, nor adulterers, nor effeminate, nor abusers of themselves with mankind, nor thieves, nor covetous, nor drunkards, nor revilers, nor extortioners shall inherit the kingdom of God." And then there comes the triumphant phrase, " *and such were some of you* " (I Corinthians 6 : 9-11). The very iniquity of Corinth was the opportunity of Christ.

IN THE WORST OF CITIES

Acts 18 : 1-11

After this Paul left Athens and came to Corinth. There he found a Jew called Aquila, who was a native of Pontus, but who had newly arrived from Italy with his wife Priscilla, because Claudius had decreed that all Jews must leave Rome. Paul went in to these people, and, because they had the same craft as he had, he worked with them; for they were leather workers to trade. Every Sabbath he debated in the Synagogue and he won over both Jews and Greeks.

When Silas and Timothy came down from Macedonia, Paul proceeded to devote himself entirely to preaching and he kept testifying to the Jews that Jesus was God's Anointed One. When they opposed him and spoke blasphemous words he shook out his raiment against them and said, " Your blood be on your own head ; I am clean ; from now on I will go to the Gentiles." So he removed from there and went to the house of a man called Titus Justus, who was a worshipper of God, and whose house was next door to the Synagogue. Crispus, the president of the Synagogue, believed in the Lord with all his household. And many of the Corinthians listened and believed and were baptized. The Lord said to Paul in a vision by night, " Stop being afraid ; go on speaking and do not be silent, because I am with you and no one will lay hands on you to hurt you, for many people are mine in this city." He settled there for a year and six months, teaching the word of God among them.

HERE we have a vivid light on the kind of life that Paul lived. Paul was a Rabbi, but according to Jewish practice, every Rabbi must have a trade. He must take no money for preaching and teaching and must make his living by his own work and his own efforts. The Jew glorified work. " Love work," they said. " He who does not teach his son a trade teaches him robbery." " Excellent," they said, " is the study of the law along with a worldly trade ; for the practice of them both makes a man forget iniquity ; but all law without work must in the end fail and causes iniquity." So we find Rabbis following every respectable trade. It meant that they never became detached scholars, and that they always knew what the life of the working-man was like. Paul is described as a tent-maker. Tarsus was in Cilicia ; in that province there were herds of a certain kind of goat with a special kind of fleece. Out of that fleece a cloth called *cilicium* was made which was much used for making tents and curtains and hangings. Doubtless Paul worked at that trade, although the word used means more than a tent-maker ; it means a leather-worker and Paul must have been a skilled craftsman. Always he gloried in the fact that he was a burden to no man (I Thessalonians 2 : 9 ; 2 Thessalonians 3 : 8 ; 2 Corinthians II : 9). But very likely when Silas and Timothy arrived they brought a present, perhaps from the Church at Philippi, which loved Paul so much ; and that present made it possible for him to devote his whole time to preaching. It was in 49 A.D. that Claudius banished all the Jews from Rome and it must have been then that Aquila and Priscilla, Paul's fellow craftsmen, came to Corinth.

Just when Paul needed it God spoke to him. Often he must have been daunted by the task that faced him in Corinth. He was a man of intense emotions and often he must have had his hours of reaction. But when God gives a man a task to do, He also gives him the power to do it. In the power and in the presence of God Paul found his courage and his strength.

IMPARTIAL ROMAN JUSTICE

Acts 18 : 12-17

> When Gallio was proconsul of Asia, the Jews got
> together to make an attack on Paul. They brought
> him to the judgment seat and said, "This man seduces
> men to worship God contrary to the Law." When Paul
> was going to speak, Gallio said to the Jews, "You
> Jews, if this were a matter of a crime or of wicked
> misbehaviour I would of course listen with patience
> to you ; but if this is a question of talk and words
> and a law observed by you, see to it yourselves. I
> have no wish to be judge of these things." So he drove
> them from his judgment seat. And they all took
> Sosthenes, the president of the Synagogue, and beat
> him before the judgment seat. And Gallio took no
> account of these things.

As usual the Jews sought to make trouble for Paul. It
was very likely that when Gallio first entered into his
proconsulship the Jews attempted to get him to act
against the Christians. They tried to influence him before
he was settled in. Gallio was famous for his kindness.
Seneca, his brother, said of him, " Even those who love
my brother Gallio to the utmost of their power do not
love him enough." He said, " No man was ever as sweet
to one as Gallio is to all." So the Jews sought to take
advantage of Gallio but Gallio was an impartial Roman.
He knew well that Paul and his friends were not guilty
of any crime, and that the Jews were trying to use him
for their own purposes. At the side of the judgment seat
were his lictors armed with their official rods and he ordered
them to drive the Jews from his judgment seat. Gallio
has of all men been most slandered. The Authorised
Version says that " Gallio cared for none of those things."
That has often been taken to mean that Gallio was detached
and uninterested ; its real meaning is that Gallio was
absolutely impartial, that he refused to allow himself to be
influenced or prejudiced, that he brought impartial Roman
justice to his task.

In this passage we see the indisputable value of a Christian life. Gallio knew that there was no fault which could be found with Paul and his friends. The only unanswerable argument for Christianity is a Christian.

THE RETURN TO ANTIOCH

Acts 18 : 18-23

> After Paul had remained there many days longer he took leave of the brethren and sailed away to Syria, and Priscilla and Aquila went with him. At Cenchrea he had his head shorn for he had a vow. They arrived at Ephesus and he left them there. He himself went into the Synagogue and debated with the Jews. They asked him to stay a longer time but he would not consent to do so, but he took leave of them saying, " God willing, I will come back to you again," and he set out from Ephesus. When he had landed at Caesarea he went up and greeted the Church and then came down to Antioch. When he had spent some time there he went away and he went successively through the Galatian country and Phrygia, establishing all the disciples.

Now Paul is on the way home. His route was by Cenchrea, the port of Corinth, and thence to Ephesus. From there he went to Caesarea ; from there he went up and greeted the Church ; that means that he went up to see the leaders of the Church at Jerusalem ; and from there he went back to Antioch from which he had started.

We are told that at Cenchrea he had his head shorn for he had a vow. When a Jew specially wished to thank God for some blessing or some deliverance he took the Nazirite vow (Numbers 6 : 1-21). If that vow was carried out in full it meant that for thirty days he neither ate meat nor drank wine ; and he allowed his hair to grow. At the end of the thirty days he made certain offerings in the Temple ; his head was shorn and the hair was burned on the altar as an offering to God. No doubt Paul was thinking of all God's goodness to him in Corinth and took this vow to show his gratitude.

We may see very clearly here how much we do not know about Paul. Acts 18 : 23—19 : 1 describe a journey of no less than 1,500 miles and it is dismissed with barely a reference. There are untold tales of heroism of Paul which we will never know.

THE THIRD MISSIONARY JOURNEY

The story of the Third Missionary Journey begins at Acts 18 : 23. It began with a tour of Galatia and Phrygia to confirm the brethren who were there. Paul then moved on to Ephesus where he remained for nearly three years. From there he went to Macedonia ; he then crossed over to Troas. From there he went by way of Miletus, Tyre and Caesarea to Jerusalem.

THE ENTRY OF APOLLOS

Acts 18 : 24-28

A Jew called Apollos, who was a native of Alexandria and a man of culture, arrived in Ephesus. He was able to use the scriptures to great effect. This man had been instructed in The Way of the Lord. He was full of enthusiasm and he told and taught the story of Jesus with accuracy, but he knew only the baptism of John. This man began to speak boldly in the Synagogue. When Priscilla and Aquila heard him they took him and more accurately explained the way of God to him. When he wished to go over to Achaea the brethren encouraged him and wrote to the disciples to make him welcome. When he had arrived he was of great help to those who had believed through grace, for he vigorously confuted the Jews in public debate, demonstrating through the scriptures that Jesus was the Anointed One.

HERE we find Christianity described as The Way of the Lord. One of the commonest titles for Christianity in Acts is The Way (9 : 2 ; 19 : 9, 23 ; 22 : 4 ; 24 : 14, 22).

That very title shows us at once that Christianity does not only mean believing certain things ; it means putting them into practice. It is not only a system of belief ; it is a way of life. It is faith, but it is a faith which issued in deeds.

Here we are introduced to Apollos. He came from Alexandria. In Alexandria there were about one million Jews. So strong were they that two out of the five wards into which Alexandria was divided were Jewish. Alexandria was the city of scholars. It was specially the place where scholars believed in the allegorical interpretation of the Old Testament. They believed that not only were the events of the Old Testament events in history but that each of them had a hidden and an inner meaning. Just because of this Apollos would be exceedingly useful in convincing the Jews because he would be able to find Christ all over the Old Testament and to prove to them that the Old Testament looked forward all the time to the coming of Jesus.

But for all that there was a lack in his training. He knew only the baptism of John. When we come to deal with the next passage we shall see more clearly what that means. But we can say now that Apollos must have seen the need for repentance ; he must have known the threat which was in John's message ; he must have recognized Jesus as the Messiah ; but as yet he did not know the good news of Jesus as the Saviour of men and of the coming of the Holy Spirit in power. He knew of the task Jesus gave men to do but he did not yet fully know of the help Jesus gave men to do it. He knew of that great call to break with the past ; but he did not yet know of that great power to live in the days to come. By the words of Aquila and Priscilla he was more fully instructed. And then Apollos, the man who knew Jesus as a figure in history, came to know Him as a living presence, and his power as a preacher must have been increased a hundredfold, for now to his knowledge he added power.

IN EPHESUS

Acts 19 is mainly concerned with Paul's work in Ephesus. Paul stayed longer in Ephesus than he stayed anywhere else for he must have been there for almost three years. Let us see then what this place Ephesus was like.

(i) Ephesus was the market of Asia Minor. In those days trade followed the river valleys. Ephesus stood at the mouth of the Cayster and therefore she commanded the richest hinterland in Asia Minor. If we read Revelation 18 : 12 and 13 we will get a description of the trade of Ephesus. She was known as " The Treasure House of Asia," and someone has called her, " The Vanity Fair of Asia Minor."

(ii) She was an Assize Town. That is to say, at certain specified times the Roman governor came there and all great cases of justice were tried. She knew the pomp, the colour, the panoply and the pageantry of Roman power and Roman justice.

(iii) She was the seat of the Pan-Ionian Games. The whole country came to these games. To be the president of these games, to be responsible for their organisation and their running was a greatly coveted honour. The men who held this high office were called *Asiarchs* and are referred to in 19 : 31.

(iv) She was the home of criminals. The Temple of Diana possessed the right of asylum. That is to say, if any criminal could reach the area round the temple he was safe. Inevitably therefore, Ephesus had become the home of the cut-throats and the swindlers and the law-breakers and the criminals of the ancient world.

(v) She was a centre of pagan superstition. She was famous for charms and spells called " Ephesian Letters." They were guaranteed to bring safety on a journey, to bring children to the childless, to bring success in love or any business enterprise. From all over the world people came to buy these magic parchments which they wore as amulets and charms.

(vi) The greatest glory of Ephesus was the Temple of Artemis. Artemis and Diana are one and the same person. Artemis is the Greek name, Diana, the Latin. It was one of the Seven Wonders of the World. It was 425 feet long by 220 feet wide by 60 feet high. There were 127 pillars, each of them the gift of a king. They were all of glittering Parian marble and 36 of them were marvellously gilt and inlaid. The great altar had been carved by Praxiteles, the greatest of all Greek sculptors. The image of Artemis was not beautiful. It was a black, squat, many-breasted figure, to signify fertility ; it was so old that no one knew where it had come from or even of what material it was made. The story was that it had fallen from heaven. The greatest glory of Ephesus was that she was the guardian of the most famous pagan temple in the world.

It was in a city like that that Paul worked and won his triumphs for Christ.

INCOMPLETE CHRISTIANITY

Acts 19 : 1-7

It happened that when Apollos was in Corinth Paul went through the upper districts and came to Ephesus and found certain disciples there. He said to them, " When you believed, did you receive the Holy Spirit ?" They said to him, " No, we never even heard that the Holy Spirit exists." He said to them, " With what, then, where you baptized ? " They said, " With the baptism of John." Paul said, " It was the baptism of repentance that John administered and he told the people that it was on Him who was to come after him that they must believe—and this is Jesus." When they heard this, they were baptized in the name of the Lord Jesus. And when Paul laid his hands on them the Holy Spirit came upon them and they spoke with tongues and prophesied. In all there were about twelve of these men.

IN Ephesus Paul met some men who were Christians but incomplete Christians. They had received the baptism of John but they did not even know that the Holy Spirit in the Christian sense of the term existed. What was the difference between the baptism of John and baptism in the name of Jesus ? Anyone who reads the accounts of the preaching of John (Matthew 3 : 7-12 ; Luke 3 : 3-11) can see one radical difference between the preaching of John and the preaching of Jesus. The preaching of John was a threat ; the preaching of Jesus was good news, it was a gospel. No one could call John's preaching good news for it threatened death and destruction. But John's preaching was a stage on the way. He himself knew that and knew that he only pointed to one still to come (Matthew 3 : 11 ; Luke 3 : 16). John's preaching was a necessary stage because there are bound to be two stages in the religious life. First, there is a stage in which we awaken to our own inadequacy and our own deserving of condemnation at the hand of God. That stage is closely allied to the time when we try to do better and inevitably fail because we try in our own strength. Second, there is the stage when we come to see that through the grace of Jesus Christ our condemnation is taken away. Closely allied with that stage is the time when we find that all our efforts to do better are strengthened and fertilised by the work of the Holy Spirit, through whom we can do what we could never do ourselves. These incomplete Christians knew the condemnation ; they knew the moral duty of being better ; but the grace of Christ and the help of the Holy Spirit they did not know. Their religion was inevitably a thing of struggle and had not reached the stage of being a thing of peace. The whole incident shows us one great truth—that without the Holy Spirit there can be no such thing as complete Christianity. Even when we see the error of our ways and repent and determine to change them we can never make the change without the help which the Spirit alone can give.

THE WORKS OF GOD

Acts 19 : 8-12

> He came into the Synagogue and for three months
> he spoke with boldness, debating and persuading
> people about the things connected with the Kingdom
> of God. When some made themselves difficult and
> would not believe, and when they spoke ill of The
> Way before the congregation he left them and with-
> drew the disciples from them and debated daily
> in the hall of Tyrannus. This went on for two years,
> so that all who lived in Asia, Jews and Greek alike,
> heard the word of God ; and God kept on doing
> extraordinary works of power through Paul's hands,
> so that sweat-bands and aprons which had touched
> his body were taken away to the sick and their diseases
> left them and the evil spirits departed.

WHEN work in the Synagogue became impossible because
of the embittered opposition Paul changed his quarters
to the hall of a philosopher called Tyrannus. There is
one Greek manuscript which adds a touch which sounds
like the additional detail an eye-witness might bring.
It says that Paul taught in that hall from the fifth to the
tenth hour, that is, from 11 a.m. to 4 p.m. Almost certainly
that is when Paul did teach. Until 11 a.m. Tyrannus would
need the hall himself, as he would after 4 p.m. In the
Ionian cities all work stopped at 11 a.m. and did not begin
again until the late afternoon. It was too oppressive to
work then. We are told that there would actually be more
people sound asleep in Ephesus at 1 p.m. than there would
be at 1 a.m. What Paul must have done was to work all
morning and all evening at his trade and teach in the midday hours. It shows us two things—the eagerness of Paul
to teach and the eagerness of the Christians to learn.
The only time they had was when others rested in the heat
of the day and they seized that time. It may well shame
many of us when we talk of inconvenient times.

It is clear that throughout this time wonderful deeds
were being done. The sweat-band was the band that a

workman wore round his head to absorb the sweat as he worked. The apron was the girdle with which a workman or servant girded himself. Yet there is an intensely significant touch here. The narrative does not say that Paul did these extraordinary deeds ; it says that God did them through Paul's hands. God, said someone, is everywhere looking for hands to use. We may not work miracles with our hands but very very certainly we can give them to God that He may work through them.

THE DEATH-BLOW TO SUPERSTITION

Acts 19 : 13-20

> Some of the itinerant Jewish exorcists tried naming the name of Jesus over those who had evil spirits. They said, " I adjure you by Jesus whom Paul preaches." There were seven sons of a certain Scaeva, a Jewish chief priest, who did this. The evil spirit answered them, " Jesus I know and Paul I understand, but who are you ? " And the man in whom the evil spirit was leaped on them and mastered them all and overpowered them so that they fled naked and battered from that house. This became known to all the Jews and Greeks who lived in Ephesus ; and awe fell upon all of them ; and the name of the Lord Jesus was magnified. Many of those who had believed came and confessed their faith and revealed the spells which they had used. Many of those who had practised magic brought their books and burned them in the presence of all. They calculated the value of them and found that it amounted to about £2,500. So the word of the Lord increased mightily and prevailed.

THIS is a vivid bit of local colour from the Ephesian scene. In those days everyone believed that illness and disease, and especially mental illness, were due to evil spirits who came and settled in a man. Exorcism was a regular trade. If the exorcist knew the name of a more powerful spirit than the spirit which had taken up residence in the afflicted person, by speaking that name he could overpower the evil spirit and make him come out. There is no reason at all to disbelieve that these things happened. The sufferers were genuinely convinced that they were possessed ; not all the exorcists were frauds ; some of them were genuinely convinced of their own powers. The human mind is a strange thing and even misguided and superstitious faith has its results in the mercy of God. When some charlatans tried to use the name of Jesus the most alarming things happened. The result was that many of the quacks, and many of those in earnest too, saw the error of their ways. Nothing can more definitely show the reality of the change than that in superstition-ridden Ephesus they were willing to burn the books and the charms which were so profitable to them. They are an example to many of us. In the most literal way they burned their boats ; they made the cleanest of clean cuts ; they never even asked how they were going to live if they abandoned the things that were their livelihood ; they made the sharp and abrupt break. It is all too true that too many of us hate our sins but cannot leave them. Even when we do seek to leave them there is the lingering and the backward look. There are times in life when treatment must be surgical, when only the clean and final break will suffice.

THE PURPOSE OF PAUL

Acts 19 : 21, 22

> When everything was completed, Paul purposed in the Spirit to go through Macedonia and go to Jerusalem. He said, " After I have been there I must see Rome too." He sent Timothy and Erastus, two of his helpers, into Macedonia and he himself extended his stay in Asia.

IT is only by the merest hint that Luke gives us an indication here of something which is filled out in Paul's own letters. Luke tells us that Paul purposed to go to Jerusalem.

Why ? At this time Paul had one great purpose. **The** Church in Jerusalem was a poor Church ; and Paul aimed to take a collection from all his Gentile Churches as a contribution to the Church at Jerusalem. We find references to this collection in I Corinthians 16 : 1ff ; 2 Corinthians 9 : 1ff ; Romans 15 : 25, 26. Paul pressed on with this scheme for two reasons. First, he wished in the most practical way to emphasize the unity of the Church. He wished them to see that they belonged to the body of Christ and that when one part of the body suffered all must help. In other words he wished to take them away from a merely congregational outlook on the Church and to give them a vision of the one universal Church of which they were part. Second, he wished to teach them practical Christian charity. Doubtless when they heard of the privations of Jerusalem they felt sorry. He wished to teach them that to feel sorry was not enough ; that that sorrow and sympathy must be translated into action. These two lessons are just as valid to-day as ever they were.

RIOT IN EPHESUS

Acts 19 : 23-41

It happened that at this time there was a great disturbance about The Way. A certain man called Demetrius, who was a silversmith and who made silver shrines of Artemis, brought very considerable profit to the craftsmen. He called them together, with the workers who were engaged in like crafts, and said, " Men, you know that our prosperity depends on this craft ; and you see and hear how not only in Ephesus but throughout nearly the whole of Asia this fellow Paul has won over and led away a great number of people telling them that gods made with hands are not gods at all. There is risk for us that not only our business may come into disrepute but also that the shrine of the great goddess Artemis may come to be held of no importance, and that she whom the whole of Asia and the civilised world worships should be robbed of her greatness." When they heard this they were filled with anger and they kept shouting, " Great is Artemis of the Ephesians." So the whole city was filled with confusion. By common consent they rushed to the theatre ; and they seized Gaius and Aristarchus who were fellow-travellers of Paul's. Paul wished to go in to the people but the disciples would not let him. Some of the Asiarchs, who were friendly to him, sent to him and urged him not to venture into the theatre. Some kept shouting one thing, and some another. The meeting was confused and the majority had no idea why it had met. At the proposal of the Jews, some of the crowd put forward Alexander. Alexander made a gesture with his hand and wished to make a defence to the people. When they realized that he was a Jew one shout arose from them all as for about two hours they kept crying, " Great is Artemis of the Ephesians. " But the town secretary quietened the crowd. He said, " Men of Ephesus, what man is there who does not know that the city of Ephesus is the temple-guardian of the great Artemis and of the image which fell from heaven ? Since these things are beyond dispute we must remain quiet and do nothing reckless. You have brought in these men who are neither temple-robbers nor blasphemers of our goddess. If Demetrius and his fellow craftsmen have a case against anyone, sessions are held and there are proconsuls. Let them bring a case against each other. If you are anxious for further steps to be taken the matter can be settled in a properly constituted assembly. For we are running the risk of being charged with a riot for this day's events for there is no cause which we could advance as a reason for this uproar." And with these words he dismissed the assembly.

THIS story, in itself a thrilling story, sheds light on the motives and minds of nearly all the characters in it. First, there is Demetrius and the silversmiths. Their trouble was that their pockets were being touched. True, they declared that they were jealous for the honour of Artemis ; but they were still more worried about their incomes. When pilgrims came to Ephesus they liked to take a souvenir home. These silversmiths were makers of little model shrines which were bought and sold as such souvenirs. Christianity was making such strides that their trade was threatened. Here is a clear case of what happened and still happens when Christianity comes up against a vested interest. Second, there is the man whom the Authorised Version calls the town clerk. He was more than that. He kept the public records ; he introduced business in the assembly ; correspondence to Ephesus was addressed to him. He was worried at the possibility of a riot. Rome was kindly, but the one thing Rome would not stand was civil disorder. If there were riots in any town Rome would know the reason why and the magistrates responsible would lose their positions. He played his part again in self-interest. True, he saved Paul and his companions but he saved them because he was saving his own skin. Third, there is Paul. There is that characteristic touch when Paul wished to face that mob and they would not let him. It never struck Paul not to face them for Paul was a man without fear. For the silversmiths and the town clerk it was safety first ; for Paul it was always safety last.

SETTING OUT FOR JERUSALEM

Acts 20 : 1-6

After the disturbance had ceased Paul sent for the disciples. He spoke words of encouragement to them and bade them farewell and departed to go to Macedonia. When he had gone through those parts and when he had spoken many a word of encouragement to them, he went into Greece. When he had spent three months there, and when he was about to set sail for Syria, a plot was made against him by the Jews. So he made up his mind to make the return journey through Macedonia. As far as Asia there accompanied him Sopatros, the son of Pyrrhus, who belonged to Beroea ; and, of the Thessalonians, Aristarchus and Secundus ; and Gaius from Derbe and Timothy ; and the men from Asia, Tychichus and Trophimus. They went on ahead and waited for us at Troas. After the days of unleavened bread we sailed away from Philippi ; and in five days time we came to them at Troas ; and there we spent seven days.

WE have already seen how Paul had set his heart on making a collection from all his churches for the Church of Jerusalem. It was to receive the contributions to that fund that Paul went into Macedonia. Here again we have an instance of how much we do not know and will never know about the story of Paul. Verse 2 says that when he had gone through those parts he came to Greece. It must have been on this occasion that he visited Illyricum (Romans 15 : 19). These few words summarize what must have been about a whole year of journey and adventure. Verse 3 tells us that when Paul was about to set sail from Greece to Syria a Jewish plot was unmasked and he changed his route to an overland way. Very likely what happened was this. Often from foreign ports Jewish pilgrim ships left for Syria to take pilgrims to the Passover. Paul must have intended to sail on such a ship. On such a ship it would have been the easiest thing in the world for the fanatical Jews to arrange that Paul should disappear overboard and never be heard of again. It was a plot like that that he discovered. Paul was a man who always walked with his life in his hands. In verse 4 we have a whole list of Paul's companions on his voyage. These men must have been delegates from the various churches charged with the duty of taking the contribution of each church to Jerusalem. They were men who were demonstrating thus early that the Church was one Church, and the need of one part of it was the challenge to and the opportunity of all the rest of it. In verse 5 we note that the narrative turns from the third person to the first person again. This is the sign that once again Luke is there and the account we are getting is an eye-witness account. Luke tells us that they left Philippi after the days of unleavened bread. The days of unleavened bread began with the day of the Passover and lasted for one week, during which the Jews ate unleavened bread in memory of their deliverance from Egypt. The time of the Passover was the middle of April.

A YOUNG MAN FALLS ASLEEP

Acts 20 : 7-12

> On the first day of the week, when we had gathered together to break bread, Paul, who was about to leave on the next day, spoke to them, and he prolonged his talk until midnight. There were many lamps in the upper room where we were assembled. A young man called Eutychus was sitting by the window. He began to be overcome by a deep sleep. While Paul was talking he was still more overcome by sleep and he fell right down from the third floor and was taken up dead. Paul went down and threw himself on him. He put his arms round him and said, " Stop making a fuss, for his life is still in him." So he went back upstairs and broke bread and ate ; and he talked with them a long time until dawn came and so he departed. And they brought in the boy alive and were greatly comforted.

So vivid is this story that it reads like what it is—an eyewitness account. Here we have one of the first accounts of what a Christian service was like. It talks twice about breaking of bread. In the early Church there were two closely related things. There was what was called the Love Feast. To it all contributed, and it was a real meal. Often it must have been the only real meal that poor slaves got all week. It was a meal when the Christians sat down and ate in loving fellowship and in sharing with each other. During it or at the end of it the Sacrament of the Lord's Supper was observed. It may well be that we have lost something of very great value when we lost the happy fellowship and togetherness of the common meal of the Christian fellowship. It marked as nothing else could the real homeliness, the real family spirit of the

Church. We see that all this happened at night. That is probably so because it was only at night, when the day's work was done, that slaves could come to the Christian fellowship. And that also explains the case of Eutychus. It was dark. In the low upper room it was hot. The many lamps and many torches made the air stuffy and oppressive. Eutychus, no doubt, had done a hard day's work before ever he came and his body was tired. He was sitting by a window to get the cool night air. Now the windows were not glass windows. They were either lattice or solid wood and opened like doors. They came right down almost to the floor and projected over the courtyard below. The tired Eutychus, overpowered by the stuffy atmosphere, succumbed to sleep and fell to the courtyard below. We must not take it that Paul spoke, as it were, even on. There would be talk and discussion but Eutychus was exhausted. Down the outside stair the crowd would pour. When they found the lad senseless they would begin to shriek and scream in the uncontrolled eastern way ; that is why Paul tells them to stop this fuss, for yet the life was in the lad. From the next verses we learn that Paul did not go with the main company ; no doubt he stayed behind to make sure that Eutychus was completely recovered from his fall. There is something very lovely about this simple picture. The whole impression is rather that of a family meeting together than of a modern congregation met in a church. Is it possible that we may have gained in what we call dignity in our Church services but that we may have lost the sense of the congregation as a real family in God ?

STAGES ON THE WAY

Acts 20 : 13-16

> But we went to the ship and set sail for Assos, for there we intended to take Paul on board for he had arranged things in this way, since he himself intended

to do that stage on foot. When we met him at Assos we took him on board and went to Mitylene. On the next day we sailed away from there and arrived opposite Chios. On the second day we crossed over to Samos, and on the next day we came to Miletus, for Paul had decided to sail past Ephesus so as not to have to spend time in Asia. For he was in a hurry, to be, if it were possible for him, in Jerusalem on the day of Pentecost.

BECAUSE Luke was with Paul we can follow Paul this time almost day by day and stage by stage. From Troas, Assos was 20 miles by road whereas it was 30 miles by sea ; and the sea journey involved the rounding of Cape Lectum against the strong prevailing north-easterly winds. Paul had ample time to make the journey on foot and to be picked up at Assos. Why did he do so ? It may well be that he wanted these days alone to nerve his spirit for the days ahead. He may well have wanted to walk alone with Christ before he faced men. Mitylene was on the island of Lesbos and Chios was on Samos and Miletus was 28 miles south of Ephesus at the mouth of the Maeander River. We have seen how Paul would have liked to have been in Jerusalem for the Passover and how the plot of the Jews hindered that. Pentecost came seven weeks later and he was eager to be there for that great feast. We may well note that though Paul had broken away from the Jews the ancestral feasts were still dear to him. Paul was the apostle to the Gentiles. His own people might hate him but in his heart there was nothing but love and yearning for them.

A SAD FAREWELL

Acts 20 : 17-38

From Miletus, Paul sent to Ephesus and summoned the elders of the Church. When they were with him he said to them, " You yourselves know how, from the first day I came into Asia, I spent all the time during which I was with you serving the Lord with all humility, and with tears, and amidst the trials that happened to me because of the machinations of the Jews. You know how I kept back nothing that was to your profit, how I did not fail to announce my tidings to you and to teach you both publicly and from house to house, testifying to both Jews and Greeks repentance towards God and faith in our Lord Jesus Christ. And now, look you, I go bound in the Spirit to Jerusalem, although I do not know what will happen to me there, except that from city to city the Holy Spirit testifies to me that bonds and afflictions await me. But I reckon my life worth nothing and I do not count it precious to myself, so be it that I may finish my course and complete the task I received from the Lord Jesus—the task of bearing witness of the good news of God. And now, look you, I know that all of you, amongst whom I went about preaching the Kingdom, will see my face no more. Therefore I affirm to you this day that I am clean from the blood of all men ; for I kept back nothing in my proclaiming to you of the whole will of God. Take heed for yourselves and take heed for all the flock in which the Spirit of God has appointed you overseers, so that you may be shepherds to the Church of God which He has rescued through the blood of His own One. I know that after I have gone away fierce wolves will enter in to you and will not spare the flock ; and from your own number there will arise men who will speak perverse things to draw the disciples away after them. Therefore be watchful and remember that for three years, day and night, I never stopped instructing each one of you with tears. And now I hand you over to God and to the word of His grace which is able to build you up, and to give you an inheritance amongst all those who have been sanctified. I coveted no man's silver or gold or raiment. You yourselves know that these very hands served my own needs and the needs of those who were with me. Always I showed you that working like this a man must help those who are in trouble and that you must remember the words of the Lord Jesus, that it was He who said, ' It is happier rather to give than to get.' "

When he had said this he knelt down and prayed with them all. And there was great lamentation among them all. They fell upon Paul's neck and kissed him repeatedly, for they were grieved most of all at the word that he had said, that they would see his face no more. And they escorted him to the ship.

It is only natural that it is not possible to make a neat analysis of a farewell speech so charged with emotion as this. But certain notes sound out. First of all Paul makes certain claims. (i) He claims that he had *spoken fearlessly.* He had told them all God's will and had kept nothing back. He had pandered neither to the fear or the favour of men. (ii) He had *lived independently.* His own hands had supplied his needs. He had neither taken nor coveted anything from any man ; and his work had not only been for his own sake but for the sake of others who were less fortunate than himself. A man may have two main objects in work—to achieve a personal independence for himself and to be able to give generously to others. (iii) *He faced the future gallantly.* He was, as he said himself, the captive of the Holy Spirit. What lay ahead he did not know, but he knew that he must face it and he knew that he could face it. But Paul also urges certain claims upon his friends. (i) He reminded them of *their duty.* They were overseers of the flock of God. That was not a duty they had chosen but a duty for which they had been chosen. The servants of the Good Shepherd must also be shepherds of the sheep. (ii) He reminded them of *their danger.* As has been said, " Eternal vigilance is the price of liberty." The infection of the world is never far away. Where truth is, falsehood ever attacks. There was a constant warfare ahead to keep the faith intact and the Church pure.

But through all this scene there runs one dominant feeling and that is the feeling of an affection and a love as deep as the heart itself. That is the feeling that should be in any Church. When love dies in any Church the work of Christ cannot do other than wither or fade. The Church of Ephesus was dear to the heart of Paul because the air and atmosphere were the air and atmosphere of love.

NO RETREAT

Acts 21 : 1-16

When we had torn ourselves away from them and had set sail, we sailed a straight course and came to Cos ; on the next day we reached Rhodes ; and from there we came to Patara. There we found a ship which was sailing across to Phoenicia and we embarked on her and set sail. After we had sighted Cyprus and had left it behind on the left hand side we sailed on to Syria and came down to Tyre, for there the ship was to discharge her cargo. We sought out the disciples and we stayed there for seven days. They told Paul through the Holy Spirit to give up his journey to Jerusalem. When we had completed the days we left and proceeded on our journey, while they all, with their wives and children, escorted us outside the city. We knelt down on the shore and prayed and bade each other farewell. Then we embarked on the ship and they returned home. We continued our voyage and arrived at Ptolemais from Tyre, and when we had greeted the brethren we stayed among them for one day. On the next day we left and came to Caesarea. We went into the house of Philip the evangelist, who was one of the Seven, and stayed with him. He had four daughters who were virgins and who prophesied. While we stayed there longer a prophet called Agabus came down from Judaea. He visited us and he took Paul's girdle and he bound his own hands and feet and said, " Thus speaks the Holy Spirit. The Jews in Jerusalem will bind the man to whom this girdle belongs like this, and they will hand him over to the Gentiles." When we heard this both we and the people of the place kept pleading with Paul not to go to Jerusalem. Then Paul answered, " What are you doing, weeping and breaking my heart ? For I am ready not only to be bound but to die in Jerusalem for the sake of the name of the Lord Jesus." Since he would not be persuaded we held our peace and said, " Let the Lord's will be done." After these days, when we had packed up, we set out on the journey to Jerusalem. Some of the disciples from Caesarea went with us. They were to bring us to Mnason, a man of Cyprus, an original disciple, with whom we were to lodge.

BY this time the narrative is speeding up and there is an inevitable atmosphere of the approaching storm as Paul comes nearer Jerusalem. Two things stand out here. (i) There is the sheer determination of Paul to go on no matter what lay ahead. Nothing could have been more definite than the warning of the disciples at Tyre and of Agabus at Caesarea, but nothing could deter Paul from the course that he had chosen. Come what may, Paul was one who marched breast forward. During one of the sieges in the Spanish Civil War there were some in one of the garrisons who wished to surrender, whereat one of their bolder comrades said, " I would rather die on my feet than live on my knees." Paul was like that. (ii) There is the very wonderful fact that wherever Paul went he found a little Christian community waiting to welcome him. If that was true in Paul's time it is still truer to-day. One of the great privileges of belonging to the Church is the fact that no matter where a man goes, to the very ends of the earth he will find in every place a community of like-minded people into which he may enter. The man who is within the family of the Church is better equipped with friends that any other man in all the world.

Agabus is an interesting figure. Jewish prophets had a certain custom. When words were inadequate they acted what they wished to say by doing something which could not fail to attract attention. As it were, they dramatised their message. There are many instances of this in the Old Testament—e.g., Isaiah 20 : 3, 4 ; Jeremiah 13 : 1-11 ; 27 : 2 ; Ezekiel 4 ; 5 : 1-4 ; I Kings 11 : 29-31.

We may note in this passage one instance in the Authorised Version where the antiquity of the language is misleading. Verse 15 says, " We took up our carriages and went up to Jerusalem." That sounds as if Paul and his friends travelled by carriage. But in the sixteenth century, used like this, the word *carriage* meant not something which carried a man but something which a man had to carry ; it meant baggage or luggage. What the sentence means is, " When we had packed up our belongings we set out for Jerusalem."

COMPROMISE IN JERUSALEM

Acts 21 : 17-26

> When we arrived in Jerusalem the brethren received us gladly. On the next day Paul along with us went to visit James ; and all the elders were present. He greeted them and recounted one by one the things which God had done among the Gentiles through his ministry. When they heard the story they glorified God. They said to him, " You see, brother, how many thousands there are among the Jews who have accepted the faith. Now they are all devotees of the Law. They have heard rumours about you which allege that you teach all the Jews who live in Gentile territory to abandon the Law of Moses and to stop circumcising their children and to stop living according to their ancestral customs. What then is to be done ? They will be bound to hear that you have arrived. So you must do what we tell you. We have four men who have taken a vow upon themselves. Take these men and be purified along with them ; and pay their expenses that they may shave their heads, and then everyone will know that the rumours they have heard about you have no truth in them but that you yourself also walk in observance of the Law. As for the Gentiles who have accepted the faith, we wrote decreeing that they should abstain from things offered to idols, from blood, from anything that has been strangled and from fornication." Then on the next day Paul took the men and was purified along with them ; he went into the Temple, and announced his intention of completing the days of purification until the offering was made for each one of them.

WHEN Paul arrived in Jerusalem he presented the Church with a problem. The leaders accepted him and saw God's hand in his work ; but rumours had been spread about him that he had encouraged Jews to forsake their ancestral faith and customs. This Paul had never done. True, he had insisted that the Jewish Law was irrelevant for the

Gentile ; but he had never sought to draw the Jew away from the customs of his fathers. The leaders saw a way in which Paul could guarantee the orthodoxy of his own faith and conduct. Four men were in the middle of observing the Nazirite vow. This was a vow which was taken in gratitude for some special goodness from the hand of God or for some special deliverance, for example in sickness. wrought by the hand of God. It involved abstention from meat and wine for thirty days, during which the hair had to be allowed to grow. It seems that sometimes at least the last seven days had to be spent entirely in the Temple courts. At the end of it certain offerings had to be brought—a year old lamb for a sin-offering, a ram for a peace offering, a basket of unleavened bread, cakes of fine flour mingled with oil, and a meat offering and a drink offering. Finally the hair had to be shorn and burned on the altar with the sacrifice. Now it is quite obvious that this was going to be a costly business. Work had to be given up and all the elements of the sacrifice had to be bought. It was quite beyond the resources of many who would have wished to undertake it. So it was considered an act of piety for some wealthier person to defray the expenses of someone who was taking the vow. That was what Paul was asked to do in the case of these four men and that was what he consented to do. By so doing he could demonstrate so that all could see it that he was himself an observer of the Law. There can be no doubt that the matter was distasteful to Paul. For him the relevancy of things like that was gone. But it is the sign of a truly great man that he can subordinate his own wishes and views for the sake of the Church. There is a time when compromise is not a sign of weakness but of strength.

A SLANDEROUS CHARGE

Acts 21 : 27-36

When the seven days were nearly completed and when the Jews from Asia had seen Paul in the Temple, they stirred up the whole mob and they attacked him shouting, " Help, men of Israel ! This is the man who teaches all men everywhere against the People, against the Law and against this place. Furthermore he has brought Greeks into the Temple and defiled this holy place." For they had seen Trophimus the Ephesian with him in the city and they thought that Paul had taken him into the Temple. The whole city was disturbed and the people rushed together. They laid hands on Paul and dragged him outside the Temple and immediately the doors were shut. While they were trying to kill him the report reached the commander of the battalion that all Jerusalem was in an uproar. He at once took soldiers and centurions and ran down to them. When they saw the commander and the soldiers they stopped beating Paul. Then the commander came up to him and arrested him and ordered him to be bound with two chains. He asked who he was and what he had done. In the crowd some shouted one thing and some another. When the commander was unable to discover the truth of the matter because of the disturbance he ordered him to be taken into the barracks. When Paul came to the steps he had to be carried by the soldiers because of the violence of the mob. For the mass of the people were following, shouting, " Kill him ! "

IT so happened that Paul's compromise led to disaster. It was the time of Pentecost. Jews were present in Jerusalem from all over the world and certain Jews from Asia were there, who no doubt knew how effective Paul's work in Asia had been. They had seen Paul in the city with Trophimus, whom they very likely knew. The business of the vow had taken Paul frequently into the Temple courts and these Asian Jews had assumed that Paul had taken Trophimus into the Temple along with him. Trophimus was a Gentile and for a Gentile to enter the Temple was a terrible thing. Gentiles could enter the Court of the Gentiles but between that court and the Court of the Women there was a barrier and into that barrier there were inset tablets with this inscription—" No man of alien race is to enter within the balustrade and fence that goes round the Temple, and if anyone is taken in the act, let him know that he has himself to blame for the penalty of death that follows." Even the Romans took this so seriously that they allowed the Jews to carry out the death penalty for this crime. The Asian Jews then accused Paul of destroying the Law, insulting the chosen people and defiling the Temple. They initiated a movement to lynch him. In the north-west corner of the Temple area there stood the Castle of Antonia which had been built by Herod the Great. At the great festivals when the atmosphere was electric it was garrisoned by a cohort of one thousand men. One thing Rome insisted on—civil order. A riot was an unforgivable sin both for the populace who staged it and the commander who allowed it. So the commander heard what was going on and came down with his troops. For Paul's own sake he had to be arrested and chained by each arm to two soldiers. In the confusion the commander was able to extract no coherent and intelligible charge from the excited mob and Paul was actually carried through the seething mob into the barracks. There was never a time when Paul was nearer death than this and it was the impartial justice of Rome which saved his life.

FACING THE FURY OF THE MOB

Acts 21 : 37-40

> When Paul was about to be brought into the barracks he said to the commander, " May I say something to you ? " He said, " Can you speak Greek ? Are you not then the Egyptian who some time ago started a revolution and led four thousand men of the Dagger-bearers out into the desert ? " Paul said, " I am a man who is a Jew, a native of Tarsus, a citizen of no mean city. I ask you, let me speak to the people." When he had given his permission to do so, Paul stood on the steps and made a gesture with his hand to the people. When a great silence had fallen he spoke to them in the Hebrew tongue.

THE Castle of Antonia was connected to the outer courts of the Temple by two flights of stairs on the northern and the western sides. As the soldiers were struggling towards the steps to reach the sanctuary of their own barracks Paul made an amazing request. He asked the captain to be allowed to address the furious mob. Here indeed is courage and here is Paul exercising his consistent policy of looking the mob in the face. The captain was amazed to hear the accents of cultured Greek coming from this man whom the crowd were out to lynch. Somewhere about 54 A.D. there had come an Egyptian to Jerusalem. He had led a band of desperate men out to the Mount of Olives with a promise that he could make the walls of the city fall down before him. The Romans had dealt swiftly and efficiently with his followers but he himself had escaped and the captain thought that Paul was this revolutionary Egyptian come back. His followers had been Dagger-bearers. These men were violent nationalists who were deliberate assassins. They concealed daggers in their cloaks and mixed with the mob and struck as they could. They were utterly reckless men. The captain thought that Paul was one of these. But Paul stated his credentials and the captain knew that whatever else Paul was he was no revolutionary thug ; and so he allowed Paul to speak. When Paul turned to speak he made a gesture for silence, and, almost miraculously, complete silence fell on that roaring mob. Nothing in all the New Testament so shows the force of Paul's personality as this silence that he commanded with gesture from the mob who would have lynched him. At that moment the very power of God flowed through Paul.

THE DEFENCE OF EXPERIENCE

Acts 22 : 1-10

" Men, brethren and fathers, listen to the defence which I now make to you." When they heard that he was addressing them in the Hebrew language they gave him still more quietness. So he said, " I am a Jew ; I was born in Tarsus ; I was brought up in this city ; I was thoroughly trained at the feet of Gamaliel in the Law of our fathers ; I was zealous for God, just as you all are to-day. I persecuted this Way to death, fettering both men and women and delivering them to prison, as the High Priest and the body of the elders bear me witness. I received letters from them and I went to the brethren at Damascus, to bring those who were there in chains to Jerusalem that they might be punished. As I was on my way, when I was coming near Damascus, about midday, suddenly it happened to me that a great light from heaven shone around me. I fell to the ground and I heard a voice saying to me, ' Saul, Saul, why are you persecuting me ? ' I answered, ' Who are you, sir ? ' And the voice said to me, ' I am Jesus of Nazareth whom you are persecuting.' Those who were with me saw the light but they did not hear the voice of the person who was speaking to me. I said, ' What am I to do, Lord ? ' The Lord said to me, ' Stand up and go to Damascus, and there you will be told about all the things that have been assigned to you to do.' "

HERE Paul makes his defence to the mob who are out for his blood ; and his defence is not to argue but to relate a personal experience, and a personal experience is the most unanswerable argument on earth. Now this defence of Paul's is in essence a paradox. It stresses two things. (i) It stresses Paul's identity with the people to whom he is speaking. He was a Jew and that Paul never forgot (cp. 2 Corinthians II : 22 ; Philippians 3 : 4, 5). He was a man of Tarsus and Tarsus was no mean city. It was one of the great ports of the Mediterranean, standing, as it did, at the mouth of the River Cydnus and being the terminus of a road which came all across Asia Minor from the far-off Euphrates. It was one of the greatest university cities of the ancient world. Still further he was a Rabbi, trained at the feet of Gamaliel who had been " the glory of the Law," and who had died only about

five years before. He had been a persecutor in his zeal
for the ancestral ways. On all these points Paul is entirely
at one with the audience to which he was speaking. (ii)
But equally this—and even more so the next passage—
stresses the difference between Paul and the audience to
which he speaks. The root difference was that he saw
Christ as the Saviour of all men and God as the lover of
the souls of all men. His audience saw God as the lover
of the Jews and of no other nation. He wanted to spread
abroad the privileges of God through all the world. They
sought to hug them to themselves and regarded the man
who would spread them abroad as sinner and a blasphemer.
And the difference was due to the fact that Paul had met
Christ face to face. The great significance of this is that
all this involves the very meaning of the word *holy*, which
is the same word which the Authorised Version translates
saint. The root meaning of the word *holy* and *saint* is
separate ; but the separation did not mean removal from
life. It meant separation for, consecration to, a special
task within life. In one sense Paul was identified with the
men to whom he spoke ; in another he was separated
from them, for though he lived among them God had
separated him for a special task. It is even so with the
Christian. He lives in the world but God has separated
him and consecrated him to a special task. He is at once
one with and different from his fellow men.

PAUL CONTINUES HIS LIFE STORY

Acts 22 : 11-21

     " Because I was not able to see because of the glory
of that light, I came into Damascus led by the hand
by those who were with me. And Ananias, a pious
man as regards the Law, a man to whose character
all the Jews who live there bear witness, came to me
and stood beside me and said, ' Brother Saul, receive
your sight again ' ; and I, in that same hour, recovered

my sight, and looked up at him. He said, ' The God of our fathers has chosen you to know His will, to see the Just One, and to hear the voice of His mouth, because you will be a witness for Him to all men of the things you have seen and heard. And now why do you wait ? Rise ; be baptized ; and wash away your sins, calling upon His name.' When I had returned to Jerusalem, and when I was praying in the Temple, it so happened that I was in a trance and I heard Him saying to me, ' Hurry ; depart speedily from Jerusalem because they will not receive your testimony about Me.' And I said, ' Lord, they know that it was I who, throughout the Synagogues, used to throw into prison and scourge those who believe in You ; and when the blood of Stephen, your witness, was shed, I too was standing by and I was agreeing to it all ; and I was guarding the clothes of those who were killing him.' And He said to me, ' Get on your way for I will send you far off to the Gentiles.' "

ONCE again Paul is stressing, to begin with, his identity with his audience. When he did reach Damascus the man who instructed him was Ananias, a man who was a devotee of the Law, and a man whom the Jews knew and agreed to be a good man. Still Paul is stressing the fact that he is no renegade ; he had not come to destroy the ancestral faith but to fulfil it. Here we have one of Luke's telescoped narratives. We must read along with this Acts 9 and Galatians 1 and we will find that it was really three years afterwards that Paul went up to Jerusalem, after his visit to Arabia and his witnessing in Damascus. Previously in Acts 9 we were told that he left Jerusalem because he was in danger of his life from the enraged Jews ; here we are told he left because of a vision. There is no real contradiction ; it is the same story told from two different points of view. The whole point Paul makes is that he did not want to leave the Jews. When God told him to do so, Paul argued. He said that his previous record would be bound to make his change all the more impressive ; but God said, No ; the Jews would never listen to him ; to the Gentiles he must go. There is a certain wistfulness here ; like His Master, Paul came unto his own and his own received him not (John I : II). Paul is literally saying, " I had a priceless gift for you ; you would not take it ; so it was offered to the Gentiles." It was not he who had hated and tried to destroy them ; it was they who had hated and rejected him.

Verse 14 is a summary not only of the life of Paul but also of the Christian life. There are three items in it. (i) *To know the will of God.* It is the first aim of the Christian man to know God's will and to obey it. (ii) *To see the Just One.* It is the aim of the Christian life daily to walk in the presence of the Risen Lord. The Christian is always saying, " Sir, I would see Jesus." (iii) *To hear the voice of His mouth.* It was said of a great preacher that in his preaching he paused ever and again as if listening for a voice. The Christian is ever listening for the voice of God above the voices of the world to tell him where to go and what to do.

THE EMBITTERED OPPOSITION

Acts 22 : 22-30

Up to this statement they listened to him, and then they cried, " Destroy such a fellow from the earth, for it is not proper for him to live." While they were shouting and waving their garments and throwing dust into the air, the commander ordered him to be brought into the barracks. He ordered him to be examined by scourging to find out why they shouted like this against him. And when they had tied him up with the thongs, Paul said to the centurion who was standing by, " Is it right for you to scourge a man who is a Roman citizen and uncondemned ? " When the centurion heard this he went to the commander and reported it. He said, " What are you going to do ? This man is a Roman citizen." The commander came to him and said, " Are you a Roman citizen ? " He said, " Yes." The commander answered " I obtained this citizenship at a great price." But

Paul said, " I was born a citizen." So at once the men who had been about to examine him stood away from him ; and the commander was afraid when he realized that he was a Roman citizen and that he had fettered him. On the next day, wishing to know the truth about the accusation made by the Jews, he released him and ordered the chief priests and the whole Sanhedrin to assemble ; and he brought Paul down and set him before them.

IT was the mention of the word Gentiles which set the mob ablaze again. It was not that the Jews objected to preaching to the Gentiles ; what they objected to was that the Gentiles were being offered privileges before they first became Jews and accepted circumcision and the Law. If Paul had preached the yoke of Judaism to the Gentiles all would have been well ; it was because he preached the grace of Christianity to them that they were enraged. They took the common way of showing their disapproval. As people did in the east they shouted and waved their garments and threw dust in the air.

The commander did not understand Aramaic and did not know what Paul had said ; but one thing he did under-stand—he must not allow a riot and he must deal at once with any man who was likely to cause a riot. So he deter-mined to examine Paul under scourging. This was not a punishment ; it was simply the most effective way of extracting either the truth or a confession. The scourge was a leathern whip studded at intervals with sharp pieces of bone and lead. Few men survived it in their right senses and many died under it. To undergo it the prisoner was tied with thongs to a whipping post with his back bent and exposed. And then Paul spoke. That might be done to aliens but not to a Roman citizen. Cicero had said, " It is a misdeed for a Roman citizen to be bound ; it is a crime for him to be beaten ; it is almost as bad as to murder a father to kill him." So Paul stated that he was a citizen. The commander was frankly terrified. Not only was Paul a citizen ; he was born free, whereas the commander had had to purchase his freedom. The commander knew that he had been on the verge of doing something which would have involved certainly his dismissal and not improbably his execution. So he loosed Paul and determined to confront him with the Sanhedrin that he might get to the bottom of this trouble.

There were times when Paul was ready to stand on his dignity ; but it was not for his own sake. He knew his task was not yet done ; he knew he must not needlessly court martyrdom nor recklessly throw his life away. Gladly he would one day die for Christ but he was too wise a man to throw his life away.

THE STRATEGY OF PAUL

Acts 23 : 1-10

Paul fixed his gaze on the Sanhedrin and said, " Brethren, I have lived before God with a completely pure conscience up to this day." The High Priest Ananias ordered those who stood by him to strike him on the mouth. Paul said to him, " God is going to strike you, you white-washed wall ! Do you sit judging me according to the Law and do you order me to be struck and so break the Law ? " Those who were standing beside him said, " Are you insulting God's High Priest ? " Paul said, " I did not know, brethren, that he was the High Priest. If I had known I would not have spoken so, for it stands written, ' You must not speak evil of a ruler of your people.' " Now Paul knew that one section of them were Sadducees and the other section were Pharisees, so he shouted out in the Sanhedrin, " Brethren, I am a Pharisee and the son of Pharisees, and I am on trial for the hope of the resurrection of the dead." When he said this a disturbance arose between the Pharisees and the Sadducees and the meeting was divided. For the Sadducees say that there is no resurrection nor angel nor spirit, while the Pharisees acknowledge both. There was a great uproar ; and some of the scribes who belonged to the party of the Pharisees stood up and argued and said, " We find no fault in this man. What if a spirit or angel has spoken to him ? " When a great disturbance was going on the commander was afraid that Paul might be torn apart by them so he ordered the guard to go down and to snatch him out of their midst and to bring him into the barracks.

THERE is a certain audacious recklessness about the conduct of Paul as he stood before the Sanhedrin ; he acted like a man who was burning his boats and who knew it. Even his very beginning was a challenge. *Brethren*, he says, and in the very word he puts himself on an equal footing with the court ; for the normal beginning for one addressing the Sanhedrin was, " Rulers of the people and elders of Israel." When the High Priest ordered Paul to be struck he himself was transgressing the Law. The Law itself said, " He who strikes the cheek of an Israelite, strikes, as it were, the glory of God." " He that strikes a man strikes the Holy One." So Paul rounds upon him calling him a white-washed wall. To touch a dead body was for an Israelite to incur ceremonial defilement ; it was therefore the custom to whitewash tombs so that none might touch one by mistake. So Paul is in effect calling the High Priest a white-washed tomb. It was indeed a crime to speak evil of a ruler of the people (Exodus 22 : 28). Paul knew perfectly well that Ananias was High Priest. But this Ananias was a notorious character. He was notorious as a glutton, a thief, a rapacious robber and a quisling in the Roman service. Paul's answer really means, " This man sitting there—I never knew a man like that could be High Priest of Israel." And then Paul made a claim that he knew would set the Sanhedrin by the ears. In the Sanhedrin there were Pharisees and Sadducees. In belief these parties were opposites. The Pharisees believed in the minutiae of the oral Law ; the Sadducees accepted only the written Law. The Pharisees believed in fate and predestination ; the Sadducees believed in free-will. The Pharisees believed in angels and spirits ; the Sadducees did not. And above all, the Pharisees believed in the resurrection of the dead ; the Sadducees did not. So Paul claims to be a Pharisee and claims that it is for the hope of resurrection from the dead he is on trial. The result was that the Sanhedrin was split in two ; and in the violent internecine argument that followed, Paul was nearly torn in pieces. To save him from violence the commander had to take him back to the barracks again. If Paul is going to go down, he is going to go down fighting to the last ditch.

A PLOT UNMASKED

Acts 23 : 11-24

On the next night the Lord stood by Paul and said, " Courage ! As you have testified for me in Jerusalem, so you must bear witness in Rome also." When it was day the Jews formed a plot and laid themselves under a vow neither to eat nor drink until they had killed Paul. There were more than forty who formed this conspiracy. They went to the chief priests and the elders and said, " We have laid ourselves under a vow to taste nothing until we have killed Paul. Now, therefore, do you lay information with the commander, so that he may bring him down to us, as if you were going to investigate his case more thoroughly ; and we are ready to kill him before he gets your length." But Paul's sister's son was there and heard the plot. So he went into the barracks and reported it to Paul. Paul called one of the centurions and said, " Take this young man to the commander for he has something to report to him." He took him and brought him to the commander and said, " The prisoner Paul called me and asked me to take this young man to you because he has something to say to you." The commander took him by the hand and took him aside privately and asked him, " What is it that you have to report to me ? " He said, " The Jews have got together to ask you to bring Paul down to the Sanhedrin to-morrow, as if they were going to make a more thorough investigation into his case. Do not you therefore agree to them for more than forty, who have taken a vow upon themselves neither to eat or drink till they have killed him, are lying in wait for him ; and they are now ready, expecting your assent." The commander dismissed the young man with instructions to tell no one that—as he said—" you have brought this information to me." He called two of his centurions and said to them, " Get ready two hundred soldiers, seventy cavalry and two hundred spearsmen to go to Caesarea at about nine o'clock in the morning. Provide baggage animals that they may mount Paul and get him through to Felix, the governor, in safety."

HERE we see two things. First, we see the lengths to which the Jews would go to eliminate Paul. Under certain circumstances the Jews regarded murder as justifiable. If a man was a public danger to morals and to life they regarded it as legitimate to eliminate him if they could. So forty men put themselves under a vow. The vow was called a *cherem*. When a man took such a vow he said, " May God curse me if I fail to do this." These men vowed neither to eat nor drink and put themselves under the ban of God until they had assassinated Paul. But fortunately their plan was laid bare by the action of Paul's nephew. Second, we see the lengths the Roman government would go to administer impartial justice. Paul was a prisoner ; he was a man lying under a charge ; but Paul was a Roman citizen and therefore the commander mobilised a small army to see Paul taken in safety to Caesarea to be tried before Felix. It is strange how the hysterical, fanatical hatred of the Jews—God's chosen people—contrasts with the cool, impartial justice of the commander—a Roman and a heathen in Jewish eyes.

THE CAPTAIN'S LETTER

Acts 23 : 25-35

The commander wrote a letter to the following effect, " Claudius Lysias to his excellency Felix, the governor —greetings ! When this man was seized by the Jews and when he was going to be murdered by them, I stepped in with the guard and rescued him, for I learned that he was a Roman citizen. As I wished to discover the charges on which they accused him, I brought him down to their Sanhedrin. I found that he was accused of some questions of their Law and was under no charge deserving of death or bonds. When it was disclosed to me that there would be a plot against the man, I immediately sent him to you, and I ordered his accusers to make their statement against him before you."

The soldiers, according to their instructions, took Paul up and brought him by night to Antipatris. On the next day they returned to barracks, leaving the cavalry to proceed with him. They came into Caesarea and delivered the letter to the governor and set Paul before him. When he had read the letter and had asked from what province he came, and when he had found out that he was from Cilicia, he said, " I will hear your case when your accusers are here also " ; and he ordered him to be kept in Herod's Praetorium.

THE seat of the Roman government was not in Jerusalem but in Caesarea. The Praetorium is the residence of a governor ; and the Praetorium in Caesarea was a palace which had been built by Herod the Great. So Claudius Lysias wrote his letter, again absolutely fair and completely impartial, and the cavalcade set out. It was 60 miles from Jerusalem to Caesarea ; Antipatris was 25 miles from Caesarea. Up to Antipatris the country was dangerous and inhabited by Jews ; after that the country was open and flat and quite unsuited for any ambush and was largely inhabited by Gentiles. So at Antipatris the main body of the troops went back and left the cavalry alone as a sufficient escort. The name of the Roman governor to whom Paul was taken was Felix and that name was a byword. For five years Felix had governed Judaea and for two years before that he had been stationed in Samaria ; he had still two years to go before he was dismissed from his post. He had begun life as a slave. His brother, Pallas,

was the favourite of Nero. Through the influence of Pallas,
Felix had risen first to be a freedman, and then to be a
governor. He was the first slave in history ever to become
the governor of a Roman province. Tacitus, the Roman
historian, said of him, " He exercised the prerogatives
of a king with the spirit of a slave." He had actually
been married to three princesses one after another. The
name of the first is not known ; the second was a grand-
daughter of Antony and Cleopatra ; the third was Drusilla,
the daughter of Herod Agrippa the First. He was completely
unscrupulous and was capable of hiring thugs to murder
his own closest supporters. It was to face a man like that
that Paul went to Caesarea.

A FLATTERING SPEECH AND A FALSE CHARGE

Acts 24 : 1-9

> Five days afterwards Ananias the High Priest came
> down with some of the elders and with a pleader
> called Tertullus. They laid information against Paul
> before the governor. When Paul was called, Tertullus
> began to accuse him in these terms, " Since through
> you we enjoy much tranquillity, and since through
> your foresight many reforms have been brought
> about for this nation, in every place and in every
> way, Felix, your excellency, we welcome it all with
> gratitude. But not to trouble you any longer, I ask
> you in your kindness briefly to hear us. When we
> had found this fellow a pest, a man who fomented
> disturbances among all the Jews throughout the
> civilised world, a man who is the ring-leader of the
> sect of the Nazarenes—and he tried to defile the
> Temple too—we arrested him. By examining him
> yourself, you can learn from him the charges of which
> we accuse him " ; and the Jews agreed with him,
> alleging that the facts were as stated.

TERTULLUS began his speech with a passage of almost
nauseating flattery, every word of which he knew and
Felix knew was quite untrue. He went on to state things

which were equally untrue. He claimed that the Jews had arrested Paul. The scene in the Temple court was far closer to being a lynching than it was to being an arrest. The charge he levelled against Paul was subtly inaccurate. The charge falls under three heads. (i) Paul was a fomenter of troubles and a pest. That classed Paul with those insurrectionaries who continually inflamed the inflammable populace into spasmodic rebellions. Tertullus well knew that the one thing that tolerant Rome would not stand was civil disorder. So vast an empire could not afford civil disorder for any spark might become a flame. Tertullus knew it was a lie but it was an effective charge. (ii) Paul was a leader of the sect of the Nazarenes. That coupled Paul with Messianic movements ; and the Romans knew what havoc false Messiahs could cause and how they could whip the people into hysterical risings which were only settled at the cost of blood. Again Rome could not afford to disregard a charge like that and again Tertullus knew that it was a lie ; but again it was an effective charge. (iii) Paul was a defiler of the Temple. The priests were Sadducees ; the Sadducees were the collaborationist party ; to defile the Temple was to infringe the rights and laws of the priests ; and the Romans, Tertullus hoped, would take the side of the pro-Roman party. The charge was that most dangerous of things—a series of half-truths and of twisted facts which were worse than lies.

PAUL'S DEFENCE

Acts 24 : 10-21

> When the governor had given him the sign to speak, Paul answered, " In the knowledge that you for many years have been a judge of this people I confidently offer my defence of my case, for you can ascertain that it is no more than twelve days since I came up to Jerusalem to worship. Neither in the Temple nor in the Synagogues nor throughout the city did

they find me arguing with anyone or collecting a crowd ; nor can they provide any truth of the accusations which they make against me. This I do admit to you—that, according to The Way, which they call a sect, I worship my ancestral God. At the same time I believe in all things that are written throughout the Law and in the prophets, and I have the same hope towards God as they themselves accept—I mean that there will be a resurrection of the just and the unjust. Because of this, I too train myself that I may always have an unharmed conscience towards God and towards men. After many years I came to bring alms and offerings to my people. In the course of these offerings they found me purified in the Temple, not with a crowd and not the centre of any disturbance. But some Jews from Asia—who ought to be present before you and who ought to be bringing whatever accusation they had against me—or let they themselves say what offence they found in me as I stood before the Sanhedrin, other than in regard to this one expression I used as I stood amongst them—' Concerning the resurrection of the dead I am on trial to-day before you.' "

BEGINNING at the passage, " But some Jews from Asia . . . " Paul's grammar goes wrong. He began to say one thing and in mid-career changed over to another and the sentence became quite disconnected. But its very disconnection shows most vividly the excitement and the tension of the scene. Paul's defence is the defence of a man whose conscience is clear—it is simply to state the facts. The tragedy was that it was when he was bringing the contributions from his churches for the poor of Jerusalem and when he was meticulously observing the Jewish Law that arrest came. One of the greatest things about Paul is that he speaks in his own defence with force, with vigour and sometimes with a flash of indignation—but there never emerge the accents of self-pity or of bitterness, which would have been so natural in a man whose finest actions had been so cruelly and deliberately misinterpreted and mis-stated.

PLAIN SPEAKING TO A GUILTY GOVERNOR

Acts 24 : 22-27

> But Felix, who had a very good knowledge of the
> facts about The Way, put them off, saying, "When
> Lysias the commander comes down I will go into
> your case." He instructed the centurion that Paul
> was to be held under guard, that he was to be allowed
> some freedom, and he instructed him not to hinder
> any of his friends from rendering him service. Some
> days after, Felix came with his wife Drusilla, who was
> a Jewess, and sent for Paul and listened to him about
> the faith in Christ Jesus. While Paul talked about
> righteousness, self-control and judgment to come
> Felix was afraid and said, " For the present, go your
> way. When I have time I will send for you." At the
> same time he hoped that money would be given him
> by Paul so he sent for him quite often and used to
> have conversation with him. At the end of two years
> Felix was succeeded by Porcius Festus ; but Felix,
> wishing to ingratiate himself with the Jews, left
> Paul a prisoner.

FELIX was not unkind to Paul but some of Paul's con-
versation and admonitions struck terror into his heart.
He came with his wife Drusilla. Now Drusilla, as we have
noted, was the daughter of Herod Agrippa the First. She
had been married to Azizus, King of Emesa. But Felix
with the help of a magician called Atomos had seduced
her from Azizus and persuaded her to marry him. It is
little wonder that when Paul presented him with the high
moral demands of God he was afraid. For two years
Paul was in prison and then Felix went too far once too
often and was recalled. There was a longstanding argument
as to whether Caesarea was a Jewish or a Greek city and
Jews and Greeks were at daggers drawn. There was an
outbreak of mob violence in which the Jews came off best.
Felix despatched his troops to aid the Gentiles. Thousands
of Jews were killed and the troops, with Felix's consent
and encouragement, sacked and looted the houses of the
wealthiest Jews in the city. The Jews did what all Roman

provincials had a right to do—they reported their governor to Rome. That was why Felix left Paul in prison. He was trying to curry favour with the Jews. It was all to no purpose. He was dismissed from his governorship and only the influence of his brother Pallas saved him from execution. So Felix passes from history, a name of shame, and from the pages of the New Testament he passes with one last act of injustice, for he left Paul in prison to please the Jews when he well knew he should have liberated him.

I APPEAL TO CAESAR

Acts 25 : 1-12

Three days after he had entered into his province, Festus went up to Jerusalem. The chief priests and the chief men of the Jews laid information before him against Paul. They urged him, asking a favour against Paul, to send for him to be brought to Jerusalem, for they were hatching a plot to murder him on the way. But Festus replied that Paul was under guard at Caesarea and that he himself would soon be leaving. " So," he said, " let your men of power come down with me, and if there is anything amiss with the man, let them make their accusations." After spending no more than eight or ten days amongst them, when he had gone down to Caesarea, he took his place on his judgment seat, and ordered Paul to be brought in. When Paul came in, the Jews who had come down from Jerusalem surrounded him ; they levelled many serious accusations against him which they were unable to prove, while Paul said in his defence, " I have committed no crime either against the Laws of the Jews, or against the Temple, or against Caesar." But Festus, with the desire to ingratiate himself with the Jews, replied to Paul, " Are you willing to go to Jerusalem and in my presence to be tried on these charges ? " But Paul said, " I am standing at Caesar's judgment seat where I ought to be tried. I have committed no crime against the Jews as you very well know ; but if I have committed some crime and if I have done something which merits death, I am not trying to beg myself off dying. But if there is nothing in the charges of which they accuse me, no one can hand me over as a favour to them. I appeal to Caesar." After Festus had conferred with his assessors, he said, " You have appealed to Caesar ; to Caesar you will go."

FESTUS was a different type from Felix ; we know very little about him, but what we do know proves that he was a just and upright man. He died after only two years in office but he died with an untainted name. The Jews tried to take advantage of him ; they tried to persuade him to send for Paul to come to Jerusalem ; for once again they had formed a plot to assassinate Paul on the way. But Festus was a Roman, with the Roman instinct for justice ; and he told them to come to Caesarea and to plead their case there. From Paul's answer we can deduce the irresponsible and malicious charges which they levelled against him. They accused him of heresy, of sacrilege and of sedition. No doubt from their point of view the first charge was true, irrelevant as it was to Roman law ; but the second two were deliberate and calculated lies. Festus had no desire to get up against the Jews in the first days of his governorship and he offered a compromise. Was Paul, he asked, prepared to go to Jerusalem and to stand his trial there while he stood by to see fair play ? But Paul knew that for him there was no such thing as fair play at Jerusalem and he took his great decision. If a Roman citizen knew that he was not getting justice in a provincial court he could appeal direct to the Emperor. Only if the man was a murderer, a pirate or a bandit caught in the act was the appeal invalid. In all other cases the local procedure had to be sisted and the claimant had to be despatched to Rome for the personal decision of the Emperor. So Paul uttered the fateful words, " I appeal to Caesar." Festus had no choice ; the appeal was valid ; and so Paul, in very different circumstances from those of which he had dreamed, had set his foot upon the first step of the road that led to Rome.

FESTUS AND AGRIPPA

Acts 25 : 13-21

WHEN some days had elapsed, Agrippa the king
and Bernice came to Caesarea to welcome Festus.
As they were staying there for some time Festus
referred Paul's case to the king. " There is a man,"
he said, " who was left behind by Felix, a prisoner.
When I was in Jerusalem the chief priests and the
elders of the Jews laid information before me concerning him and asked for his condemnation. I
replied to them that it is not the custom of the Romans
to grant any man's life as a favour before the accused
meets his accusers face to face and receives an opportunity to make his defence against their charge. So
when they came down here I made no delay, but on
the next day I took my seat on my judgment seat
and ordered the man to be brought in. The accusers
rose and brought against him none of the accusations
of crime which I was expecting ; but they had an
argument with him about their own religion and about
someone called Jesus who was dead and whom Paul
insists to be alive. I did not know what to make of
the dispute about these matters so I asked him if
he was willing to go to Jerusalem and to be tried
there on these charges ; but Paul appealed and
demanded to be held for His Majesty's investigation
and decision ; so I ordered him to be held until I
shall remand him to Caesar."

AGRIPPA was still king of a quite small part of Palestine,
which included Galilee and Peraea ; but he knew quite
well that he held even that limited realm by grace of the
Romans. They had put him there and they could just as
easily remove him. It was therefore his custom to pay
a courtesy visit to the Roman governor when he entered
upon his province. Bernice was a sister of Drusilla
who was the wife of Felix and she was also a sister of
Agrippa himself. Now Festus knew that Agrippa had the
most intimate knowledge of Jewish faith and belief and
practice so not unnaturally he proposed to discuss Paul's
case with him. He gave Agrippa a characteristically
impartial review of the situation as it existed at that

moment ; and now the stage was set for Paul to plead his case and bear his witness before a king. Jesus had said, " Ye shall be brought before governors and kings for My sake " (Matthew 10 : 18). The hard prophecy had come true ; but the promise of help (Matthew 10 : 19) was also to come abundantly true.

FESTUS SEEKS MATERIAL FOR HIS REPORT

Acts 25 : 22-27

Agrippa said to Festus, " I too would like to hear the man." " To-morrow," he said, " you will hear him." So on the next day Agrippa and Bernice came with much pomp ; and when they had come into the audience-chamber with the captains and the leading men of the city Paul was brought in. So Festus said, " King Agrippa and all who are here present with us, you see this man, concerning whom the whole community of the Jews kept petitioning me both in Jerusalem and here, crying out that he ought not to be allowed to live any longer. I understood that he had done nothing to merit death. But when this man himself appealed to His Majesty, I gave judgment to send him. I have nothing definite to write to my lord about him. So I have brought him in before you, and especially before you, King Agrippa, so that, when investigation has been made, I may have something to write. For it seems to me unreasonable to send a prisoner and not to send the charges against him."

FESTUS had got himself into a difficulty. It was Roman law that if a man appealed to Caesar and was sent to Rome there must be sent with him a written account of the case and of the charges against him ; and Festus' problem was that, as far as he could see, there was just no charge to send. It was to find some charge that this whole meeting was convened. There is no more dramatic scene in all the New Testament. It was with pomp that Agrippa and Bernice had come. They would have on their purple robes of royalty and the gold circlet of the crown on their brows. Doubtless Festus, to do honour to the occasion, had donned the scarlet robe which a governor wore on state occasions. Close at hand there must have stood Agrippa's suite and all round the most influential figures of the Jews. Close by Festus there would stand the captains in command of the five cohorts which were stationed at Caesarea ; and in the background there would be a solid phalanx of the tall Roman legionaries on ceremonial guard. It was into a scene like that there came Paul, the little Jewish tent-maker, with his hands in chains ; and yet from the moment he speaks it is Paul who dominates the scene. There are some men who have an element of power. Julian Duguid tells how he once crossed the Atlantic in the same ship as Sir Wilfred Grenfell. Grenfell was not a particularly imposing figure to look at ; but Duguid tells that when Grenfell entered one of the ship's rooms he could tell he was there without looking round, because a wave of power emanated from the man. When a man has Christ in his heart and God at his right hand he has the secret of power. Of whom then shall he be afraid ?

THE DEFENCE OF A CHANGED MAN

Acts 26 : 1-11

Agrippa said to Paul, " You have permission to speak on your own behalf." Then Paul stretched out his hand and began his defence. " With regard to the charges made against me by the Jews, King Agrippa, I count myself fortunate to be about to state my defence before you, especially because you are an expert in all Jewish customs and questions. Therefore I ask you to give me a patient hearing. All the Jews know my way of life from my youth, which from the beginning I lived amongst my people in Jerusalem. They already know from of old, if they are willing to testify to it, that I lived as a Pharisee according to the strictest sect of our religion; and now it is for the hope of the promise that was made to our fathers that I stand on trial, that hope to which our twelve tribes hope to attain, earnestly worshipping God day and night. It is for that hope, your Majesty, that I am accused. Why should you judge it to be incredible if God raises the dead ? It is true that I myself thought it right to do many things in opposition to the name of Jesus of Nazareth ; and this I did in Jerusalem. When I had received authority from the chief priests I shut up many of the saints in prison ; and when they were executed I gave my vote against them. Often throughout all the Synagogues I took vengeance on them and I tried to force them to blaspheme. In my insane fury against them I even extended this persecution of them to cities abroad."

ONE of the extraordinary things about the great characters in the New Testament story is that they were never afraid to confess what once they had been. Here in the presence of the king, Paul frankly and freely confesses that there was a day when he had tried to eliminate the name of Christ and to blast the Christians out of existence. There was a famous evangelist and preacher called Brownlow North. He too was a changed man and in his early days he had lived a life that was anything but Christian. Once, just before he was to enter the pulpit to preach in a church in Aberdeen, he received a letter. This letter informed him that its writer had evidence of some disgraceful thing which Brownlow North had done before he became a Christian ; and it went on to say that the writer proposed to interrupt the service and to tell the whole congregation of that sin if Brownlow North preached. Brownlow North took the letter into the pulpit ; he read it to the congregation ; he told of the thing that once he had done ; and then he told them that the charge was absolutely true but that Christ had changed him and that Christ could do the same for them. He used the very evidence of his shame to turn it to the glory of Christ. Denney used to say that the great function of Christianity was in the last analysis to make bad men good. The great Christians have never been afraid to point to themselves as living

and walking examples of the power of Christ. The gospel to
them was not a form of words ; it was not a form of intellectual belief ; it was a power unto salvation. It is true that
a man can never change himself ; but it is also gloriously
true that what he cannot do, Jesus Christ can do for him.

We note how in this passage Paul insists that the centre
of his whole message was the Resurrection. His story
and his witness were not of someone who had lived and
died but of One who was gloriously present and alive for
evermore. For Paul every day in life was Easter Day.

SURRENDER FOR SERVICE

Acts 26 : 12-18

> " When, in these circumstances, I was on my way to
> Damascus with authority and commission from the
> chief priests, as I was on the road at midday, I saw,
> your Majesty, a light from heaven, more brilliant
> than the sun, shining round about me and my fellow-
> travellers. When we had fallen to the ground, I
> heard a voice saying to me in the Hebrew language,
> ' Saul, Saul, why are you persecuting me ? It is
> hard for you to kick against the spikes.' I said, ' Who
> are you, sir ? ' The Lord replied, ' I am Jesus whom
> you are persecuting. But up ! and stand upon your
> feet ! For this is why I have appeared to you—to
> appoint you a servant and a witness of how you have
> seen Me and of further visions you will have ; for I
> am choosing you from the People and from the Gentiles,
> to whom I am sending you to open their eyes, to turn
> them from darkness to light and from the power of
> Satan to God, that they may receive forgiveness of
> sins and a share amongst those who have been sanctified
> by faith in Me.' "

THIS is a passage which is full of interest. (i) The Greek
word *apostolos* literally means, *one who is sent forth*. For
instance, an ambassador who is sent forth by his country
is an *apostolos* or *apostle*. Now the interesting thing is
that an emissary of the Sanhedrin was technically known

as the *apostolos* of the Sanhedrin. And so we see that Paul began this journey as the apostle of the Sanhedrin of the Jews and ended it as the apostle of Christ. (ii) We learn from this that Paul was pressing on with his journey *at midday*. Unless a traveller was in a really desperate hurry he did not travel through the middle of the day but rested during the midday heat. So we see how Paul was driving himself on this mission of persecution. Beyond a doubt he was trying by violent action to still the doubts that were in his heart. (iii) The Risen Christ tells Paul that it was hard for him to kick against the pricks. When a young ox was first yoked it resented it and tried to kick his way out of the yoke. If it was yoked to a one handed plough the ploughman held in his hand a long staff with a sharpened end which he held close to the ox's heels so that every time it kicked it was jagged with the spike. If it was yoked to a wagon, at the front of the wagon there was a bar studded with wooden spikes and if it kicked it only hurt itself. The young ox had to learn submission to the yoke the hard way and so had Paul. But further verses 17 and 18 give us a perfect summary of what Christ does for men. (*a*) *He opens their eyes.* When Christ comes into a man's life he enables him to see the things he never saw before. The eyes which were bound to earth suddenly see the glory of heaven. The eyes which were fixed on self suddenly look with love on others. (*b*) *He turns them from the darkness to the light.* Before a man has met Christ it is as if he had been facing the wrong way. Because he had his back to the light he walked in the shadows ; but now he is walking towards the light and his way is clear before him. (*c*) *He transfers him from the power of Satan to the power of God.* Whereas once evil had him in thrall he is now the son of God with all God's triumphant power to enable him to live not as the slave of sin but in victorious goodness. (*d*) *He gives him forgiveness of sins and a share with the sanctified.* For the past, the penalty of sin is broken; for the future, life is recreated and purified. He is delivered both from the fear of the past and the fear of the future.

A TASK ACCEPTED

Acts 26 : 19-23

" Therefore, King Agrippa, I was not disobedient to the heavenly vision. But first of all to those in Damascus, and to Jerusalem, and throughout the whole land of Judaea and to the Gentiles, I brought the message to repent and turn to God and do deeds to match their repentance. Because of this the Jews seized me in the Temple and tried to do away with me. So then because I have received the help of God up to this day, I stand bearing witness to great and small, saying nothing beyond those things which both the prophets and Moses said would happen, that the Anointed One must suffer, that as a consequence of His resurrection from the dead He must be the first to bring the tidings of light to the People and to the Gentiles."

HERE we have a vivid summary of the substance of the message which Paul preached. (i) He called on men to *repent*. The Greek word for *repent* literally means *to change one's mind*. It means to realize that the kind of life we were living was wrong and to start out on life with a completely new set of values and principles. It means the realization that life must be changed. To that end, it involves two things. First, it involves *sorrow*. It means a sorrow as deep as the deepest depths of the heart that ever we were what we have been, and that ever we did what we have done. Second, it means a new *resolve* a determination that by the grace of God we will be changed. It is a break with the past and a dedication to God. (ii) He called on men *to turn to God*. So often we have our backs to God. It may be in thoughtless, unremembering disregard; it may be because we have deliberately gone out to the far countries of the soul. But, however that may be, it means that we face God in such a way that the God we forgot or whom we banished from life becomes the one person who fills all our horizon and who dominates all our life. The God who was nothing to us becomes the God who is everything to us. (iii) He called on men *to do deeds to match their repentance.* The proof of repentance and the proof of turning to God is a certain kind of life. But mark this—these deeds, this new quality, are not the reaction of someone whose life is governed by a new series of *laws* for the keeping of which he is answerable to a judge ; that would simply be a new legalism ; they are the result of a new *love.* They come from the fact that when a man realizes the love of God in Jesus Christ he must say, " I cannot stay the way I am ; I must give all my life to one great effort to deserve that love." He knows now that if he sins he does not break God's law ; he breaks God's heart.

A KING IMPRESSED

Acts 26 : 24-31

> As Paul was making his defence, Festus cried out, " Paul, you are mad. Much learning has turned you to madness." But Paul said, " I am not mad, Festus, your Excellency, but I am uttering words of truth and sense. The king has knowledge of these things and it is to him that I boldly talk ; for I do not think that any of these things are escaping him ; for this was not done in a corner. King Agrippa, do you believe the prophets ? I know you do." Agrippa said, " You surely think that you are not going to take long to persuade me to be a Christian." Paul answered, " I could pray that, whether it takes short or long, not only you but also all who are listening to me to-day were such as I am, apart from these fetters." The king and the governor and Bernice and those who were sitting with them rose up ; and when they had withdrawn they kept saying to each other, " This man does nothing which merits death or fetters." And Agrippa said to Festus, " This man could have been released if he had not appealed to Caesar."

It is not so much what is actually said in this passage which is interesting as the whole atmosphere which the reader can feel behind it. Paul was a prisoner. At that very moment he was wearing his fetters, as he himself makes clear. And yet the whole atmosphere is that he is the dominating personality in the scene. Festus does not speak to him as a criminal. No doubt he knew Paul's record as a trained rabbi ; no doubt he had seen Paul's room scattered with the scrolls and the parchments which were the earliest Christian books. Paul to him is not a criminal ; at the worst he is a man whose mind has become unbalanced with too much study. As for Agrippa, when Paul speaks to him, it is rather Agrippa who is on trial than Paul. And the end of the matter is that a rather bewildered company of people cannot see any real reason why Paul should be tried in Rome or anywhere else. The whole incident is an outstanding example of the power of personality. This one man Paul has in him a power which raises him head and shoulders above all others in any company. The word which is used for the power of God in Greek is the word *dunamis*. It is the word from which *dynamite* comes. It is the word from which the man who has Christ in his heart and the Risen Christ at his side need fear no man. The dignity of God is on him and beside that human dignities are pale and bloodless things.

THE LAST JOURNEY BEGINS

Acts 27 : 1-8

When it was decided that we should sail for Italy, they handed over Paul and some other prisoners to a centurion of the Cohort Augusta called Julius. When we had embarked upon a ship of Adramyttium, which was bound for the ports along the coast of Asia Minor, we set sail, and Aristarchus, a Macedonian from Thessalonica, was with us. The next day we put in at Sidon. Julius treated Paul kindly and allowed him

to visit his friends and to receive their attention. We put out from there and sailed under the lea of Cyprus because the winds were against us. When we had crossed the sea, coasting along the shores of Cilicia and Pamphylia, we reached Myra in Lycia. There the centurion found an Alexandrian vessel bound for Italy and embarked us on her. When we were making slow progress for many days, and when we had with difficulty arrived off Cnidus, because the wind was unfavourable, we sailed under the lea of Crete off Salmone. With difficulty we sailed along the coast and reached a place called Fair Havens, to which the town of Lasea is near.

Now Paul has embarked upon his last journey. Two things must have lifted up his heart. One was the kindness of a stranger, for all through the voyage Julius, the Roman centurion, treated Paul with a kindness and consideration which were more than mere courtesy. He is said to have belonged to the Augustan Cohort. It may be that that was a special corps who acted as liaison officers between the Emperor and the provinces. If that is so Julius must have been a man of long experience and with an excellent military record. It may well be that when Paul and Julius stood face to face one brave man recognized another. The other uplifting thing was the devotion of Aristarchus. It has been suggested that there was only one way in which Aristarchus could have accompanied Paul on this last journey and that was by enrolling himself as Paul's slave. It is very probable that Aristarchus chose to act as the slave of Paul rather than to be separated from him—and loyalty can go no further than that.

The voyage began by coasting up to Sidon. The next port of call was Myra but things were difficult. The prevailing wind at that time of year was the west wind and they could only make Myra by slipping under Cyprus and then following a zigzag course up the coast. At Myra they found a ship from Alexandria bound for Rome. She would be a corn ship, for Egypt was the granary of Italy. If we look at the map we can see what a long way round she had had to take ; but these strong west winds made the direct journey impossible. To sail direct to Italy she would have set out straight across the Agean Sea but the strong west wind made that impossible, and after many days of beating against the wind she slipped under the lee of Crete, and came to a little port called Fair Havens.

IN PERIL ON THE SEA

Acts 27 : 9-20

Since a considerable time had elapsed, and since it was now no longer safe for sailing because the Fast was already past, Paul offered his advice. " Gentlemen," he said, " I see that this voyage is going to be fraught with injury and much loss not only to the cargo and to the ship but also to our own lives." But the centurion was persuaded by the master and the owner rather than by what Paul said. Since the harbour was not suitable to winter in, the majority proposed the plan of sailing from there, to see if they were able to reach Phoenice and to winter there. Phoenice is a harbour in Crete which faces south-west and north-west. When a light southerly wind blew they thought that their purpose was as good as achieved ; so they weighed anchor and coasted close in along the shores of Crete. But soon a tempestuous wind called Euraquilo rushed down from it upon them. When the ship was caught by it and when she could not keep her head to the wind, we yielded to the wind and scudded before it. When we had run under the lea of a little island called Cauda we had great difficulty in getting the dinghy under control. They used their lifting tackle to get it on board and they frapped the ship. Because they were afraid that they would be cast on to the Syrtis Sands they loosed the gear and away they were driven. When they were making very heavy weather on the next day they began to throw equipment overboard ; and on the third day with their own hands they jettisoned the ship's spare gear. When neither sun nor stars were seen for many days, and when a great storm was raging, at last all hope that we should be saved was taken away.

IT is quite certain that Paul was the most experienced traveller on board that ship. The Fast that is referred to is the Jewish Day of Atonement and on that year that day fell in the first half of October. Now according to the navigational practice of the time, sailing was considered doubtful after September and impossible by November. It has always to be remembered that the ancient ships had neither sextant or compass and in cloudy and dark weather they had no means of finding their way. It was Paul's advice that they should winter in Fair Havens where they were. As we have seen, the ship was an Alexandrian corn ship. The owner would be rather the contractor who was bringing the cargo of corn to Rome. The centurion, being the senior officer on board, had the last word. It is significant that Paul, the prisoner under arrest, had every chance to say his say when counsel was being taken. But Fair Havens was not a very good harbour nor was it near any sizable town where the winter days might be passed by the crew ; so the centurion rejected Paul's advice and took the advice of the master and the contractor to sail farther along the coast to Phoenice which was a more commodious harbour and a bigger town. A very unexpected south wind made the plan seem easy ; and then there struck them the terrible wind from the north-east. It was a gale and the peril was that if they could not control the ship they would inevitably be blown on the Syrtis Sands which were off North Africa and which were the graveyard of many a ship. They have been called " The Goodwin Sands of the Mediterranean." By this time they had managed to get the dinghy, which had been towed behind, on board, in case it should either become water-logged or dashed to pieces against the ship. They began to throw out all spare gear to lighten the ship. With the stars and the sun shut out they did not know where they were and the terror of the Syrtis Sands gripped them so that they abandoned hope

BE OF GOOD CHEER

Acts 27 : 21-26

> Since they had been without food for a long time Paul stood up in the midst of them and said, "Gentlemen, you should have obeyed me and you should not have sailed from Crete and so you would have avoided this injury and loss. So now I advise you to keep your hearts up. There will be no loss of life among you, but only the ship. For this night there stood beside me the Angel of God, whose I am and whom I serve, saying, 'Have no fear, Paul ; you must stand before Caesar ; and lo, God has granted you all those who are sailing with you.' So, gentlemen, be in good heart ! For I trust God that things will turn out as it has been told to me ; but we must be cast upon an island."

THE peril of the ship was by this time really desperate. These corn ships were not small ships. They could be as large as 140 feet long and 36 feet wide and of 33 feet draught. But in a storm they had certain grave disadvantages. They were the same at the bow as at the stern, except that the stern was swept up like a goose's neck. They had no rudder like a modern ship, but were steered with two great paddles coming out from under the stern on each side. They were therefore hard to manage. Further, they had only one mast and on that mast one great square sail, made sometimes of linen and sometimes of stitched hides. With a sail like that they could not sail into the wind. And worst of all, the single mast and the great sail put such a strain on the ship's timbers in a gale that often the timbers of such ships started and they foundered at sea. It was to avoid that that they frapped the ship. That means that they passed hawsers under the ship and drew them tight round the ship with their winches so that they literally held the ship together like a tied up parcel. It can easily be seen what peril they were in. And then an amazing thing happened, for it is quite clear that Paul took command. The prisoner had become the captain, for he is the only man with any courage left. It is told that once on one of his voyages the crew of Sir Humphrey Gilbert's ship were terrified ; they felt that they were sailing right out of the world in the mists and the storms and the unknown seas. They came to him and asked him to turn back. He would not do it. " I am as near to God, by sea," he said, " as ever I was by land." The man of God is the man whose courage stands when terror invades the hearts of others. He is a leader of men because he himself is led by God.

HOPING FOR THE DAY

Acts 27 : 27-38

When the fourteenth night came and when we were drifting across in the Adriatic, in the middle of the night the sailors suspected that some land was approaching them. They took a sounding and found twenty fathoms. Since they were afraid that they would be cast up on rough places they cast four anchors out of the stern and hoped for the day. When the sailors were trying to escape from the ship, and when they were lowering the dinghy into the sea on the pretext of being about to send out anchors from the bow, Paul said to the centurion, " If these do not stay in the ship you cannot be saved." Then the soldiers cut the dinghy's ropes and let her fall away. When it was nearly day, Paul urged all of them to take some food. " To-day," he said, " is the fourteenth day you have spent waiting without food and have taken nothing. So I urge you to take some food for this is for your health ; for not a hair of the head of anyone of you will be lost." When he had said this and when he had taken bread he gave thanks to God before them all and brake it and began to eat. All of them were in good heart and took food. And we who were in the ship were two hundred and seventy-six souls in all ; and when they were satisfied with food they lightened the ship by casting the corn into the sea.

By this time they had lost all control of the ship. She was drifting, broadside on, across the Adriatic ; and since there were no stars and no sun to see they could not tell where they were. In the darkness they heard the crash of breakers on some distant shore ; they cast out sea anchors from the stern to slacken the drifting speed of the ship lest she should be cast on the rocks that they could not see. It was then that Paul took the action of a commander. The sailors planned to sail away in the dinghy, which would have been quite useless for two hundred and seventy-six people ; but Paul frustrated their plan. The ship's company must sink or swim together. And then there follows a most human and suggestive episode. Paul insisted that they should eat. Paul was a man of visions and a man of God ; but Paul was also an intensely practical man. He had not the slightest doubt that God would do His part but he also knew that men must do theirs. It could never be said of Paul as it was said of some people that " they were so heavenly minded that they were of no earthly use." He knew that hungry men are not efficient men ; and so he gathered the ship's company around him and made them eat. As we read the narrative, into the tempest of the storm there seems to come a strange calm. The man of God has somehow made others sure that God was in charge of things. The most useful people in the world are those who, being themselves brave, help others to be brave ; and who, being themselves calm, bring to others the secret of confidence. Paul was like that ; and all the followers of Jesus must be steadfast when others are in turmoil.

ESCAPE FROM THE DEEP

Acts 27 : 39-44

> When day came they did not recognize the land ; but they saw a bay with a beach, on which they purposed, if it was possible, to run the ship ashore. They loosed the anchors and let them go into the sea and at the same time they loosed the lashings of the rudder

paddles, and they set the foresail to the wind and made for the beach. When they were cast into a place where two seas met they beached the ship ; and the bow remained fast and immovable but the stern was being broken up by the surf. The soldiers had a plan to kill the prisoners lest any should swim away and escape ; but the centurion, wishing to save Paul, stopped them from their purpose. He ordered those who could swim to throw themselves overboard first and to get to land ; as for the rest, he ordered some to go on planks and some on pieces of the ship. So it happened that all came safely to the land.

ONCE again the fine character of this Roman centurion stands out. The soldiers wished to kill the prisoners lest they should escape ; and it is difficult to blame them, because it was Roman law that if a man escaped, his guard must undergo the sentence and the penalty which the escaped prisoner would have undergone ; but the centurion stepped in and saved Paul's life and the other prisoners with him. So this tremendous story comes to an end with a sentence which is like a sigh of relief. The ship's company was saved ; and the fact remains that they owed their lives to Paul. One thing is clear—if Paul had not been the greatest of missionaries he could have been one of the greatest men of action the world has ever seen, for Paul was first and foremost a man in the fullest sense of the term.

WELCOME AT MALTA

Acts 28 : 1-6

When we had been brought safely to shore, then we recognized that the island was called Malta. The natives showed us quite extraordinary kindness for they lit a bonfire and they brought us all to it because of the rain which had come on and the cold. When Paul had twisted up a faggot of sticks and when he had placed it on the fire, a viper came out of it because of the heat, and fastened on his hand. When the natives saw the snake hanging from his hand they said to each other, " This man must be a murderer, and, although he has been rescued from the sea, justice has not allowed him to live." But Paul shook the snake off into the fire and took no harm. They stood waiting for him to swell up or suddenly to fall down dead ; and when they had waited expectantly for a long time and when they saw that nothing untoward was happening to him, they changed their minds and began to say that he was a god.

IT was upon the island of Malta that Paul and the ship's company were cast. The Authorised Version is a little unkind to the Maltese. It calls them the *barbarous* people. It is true that the Greek calls them *barbaroi* ; but to the Greek the barbarian was a man who said *bar-bar*, that is to say, the man who spoke an unintelligible foreign language and not the flexible and beautiful Greek tongue. We come nearer to the meaning when we simply call them the *natives*. This passage sheds vivid little side-lights on the character of Paul. For one thing, there is the lovely and the homely touch that Paul was a man who could not bear to be doing nothing ; he had to make himself useful ; there was a bonfire to be kindled and kept alight and Paul was there gathering brushwood for it. Once again we see that for all Paul's visions he was an intensely practical man ; and still more, we see that Paul, great man though he was, was not ashamed to be useful in the smallest thing as well as the greatest. It is told that Booker Washington in his youth walked hundreds of miles to one of the few universities which took in negro students. When he got there he was told that the classes were full. He was offered a job at making beds and sweeping floors. He did not turn up his nose at it ; he took it ; and he swept those floors and made those beds so well that before very long they took him as a student and he went on to become the greatest scholar and administrator of his people. It is only the little man who refuses the little task. Still further, we see Paul as a man cool and unexcited. In one of his bundles of brushwood there was a torpid viper ; the heat wakened it and it fastened itself to his hand. It is difficult to tell whether this is a miraculous happening or not. It is a fact that nowadays at least there is no such thing as a poisonous snake in Malta ; and in Paul's time there was a snake very like a viper but quite harmless. It is far more likely that Paul shook off the snake before it had time to bite or to pierce his skin. In any event he seems to have done the whole thing as if it did not matter ; and it certainly looked to the Maltese like a miracle. Clearly at any rate Paul was a man who did not fuss !

HELP AND HEALING

Acts 28 : 7-10

> In the neighbourhood of that place there were estates which belonged to the Chief of the island, who was called Publius. He welcomed us and hospitably entertained us for three days. It so happened that Publius' father was lying ill, in the grip of intermittent attacks of fever and of dysentery. Paul went to visit him. He prayed and laid his hands on him and cured him. When this happened the rest of the people in the island who had ailments kept coming and being cured. So they heaped honours upon us and when we left they gave us supplies for our needs.

IT seems that in Malta the Chief of the island was a title ; and Publius may well have been the chief Roman representative for that part of the island. His father was ill and Paul was able to exercise his healing gift and to bring him relief. But in verse 9 there is a very interesting possibility. That verse says that the rest of the people who had ailments came and *were healed*. The word used is the word for *receiving medical attention* ; and there are scholars who think that this can well mean, not only that they came to Paul, but that they came to Luke and that Luke, the doctor, the beloved physician, gave them of his skill. If that be so this is one of the most interesting passages in the New Testament ; because it would give us the earliest picture of the work of a *medical missionary* that we possess ; and it would be the first account of a kind of scene that has been re-enacted all over the world times without number ever since. There is a poignant thing here. Paul could exercise the gift of healing ; and yet Paul had forever to bear about with him the thorn in the flesh. He healed others while he could not heal himself. Like his Master, in another sense, he saved others when he could not save himself. Many a man has brought to others a gift which was denied to him. Beethoven, for instance, gave to the world immortal music which he himself, being stone-deaf, never heard. It is one of the wonders of grace that such men did not grow bitter but were content to be the channels of gifts which they themselves could never share.

SO WE CAME TO ROME

Acts 28 : 11-15

> After three months we set sail on an Alexandrian ship which had wintered in the island, the figure-head of which was The Heavenly Twins. We landed at Syracuse and stayed there for three days. From there we sailed round and arrived at Rhegium ; and, after one day, when the south wind had sprung up, we made Puteoli in two days. There we found brethren and were invited to stay amongst them for seven days ; and so we came to Rome. When the brethren had received news about us, they came from there to meet us, as far as Apii Forum and the Three Taverns. When Paul saw them he thanked God and took courage.

AFTER three months Paul and the ship's company managed to get passages for Italy on another corn ship which had wintered in Malta. In those days ships had figure-heads. Two of the favourite gods of sea-faring folk were The Heavenly Twins, Castor and Pollux ; and this ship had carved images of them as its figure-head. This time the voyage was as prosperous as the previous one had been disastrous. Puteoli was the port of Rome. There must have been tremors in Paul's heart for now he was on the very threshold of the capital of the world, immortal Rome. How would a little Jewish tent-maker fare in the greatest city in the world ? To the North there lay the port of

Misenum where the Roman fleets were stationed ; and as he saw the warships in the distance Paul must have thought of the might of Rome. Nearby there were the beaches of Baiae which was the " Brighton of Italy," with its crowded beaches and the coloured sails of the yachts of the wealthy Romans. Puteoli, with its wharves and its store-houses and its granaries and its ships, has been called the " Liverpool of the ancient world." For once there must have been a catch at the heart of Paul as he alone faced Rome. And then something happened. Apii Forum is 43 miles from Rome and The Three Taverns 33 miles from Rome. They were on the great Appian Way which lead from Rome to the coast. And there came a deputation of the Roman Christians to meet him. What is very suggestive is this, that the word that the Greek uses for the meeting is the word that is used for a city deputation going out to meet a general or a king or a conqueror. They came to meet Paul as one of the great ones of the earth ; and Paul thanked God and took courage. What was it that so specially lifted up the heart of Paul ? Surely the answer is clear—the sudden realisation that he was not alone. The Christian is never alone. (i) He has the consciousness of the unseen cloud of witnesses around him and about him. He knows that he walks in a great succession on which all the saints look down and on the very road the saints have trod. (ii) He has the consciousness of belonging to a world-wide fellowship. He is a member of the Church of Christ whose boundaries are the world. Wherever he goes there will be a circle of people with whom he can be at home. (iii) He has the consciousness that wherever he goes there is God. The old mapmakers used to write on their maps in unknown lands, " Here be dragons ; here be burning fiery sands." The Christian can write of every place, " Here is God." (iv) He has the certainty that his Risen Lord is with him. He has the promise, " Lo, I am with you alway " ; and that is the promise of One who never breaks His word.

UNSYMPATHETIC JEWS

Acts 28 : 16-29

When we arrived in Rome, permission was given to Paul to stay in his own house, with the soldier who was his guard. After three days it happened that he invited the leaders of the Jews to come to see him. When they had assembled he proceeded to say, " Brethren, although I have done nothing against the People or against our ancestral customs, I was given over as a prisoner into the hands of the Romans from Jerusalem. When the Romans had investigated my case they wished to release me because there were no grounds which could be made a capital charge against me. When the Jews objected to my release I was compelled to appeal to Caesar, not that I had any accusation to make against my nation. It is for this reason that I have invited you to come to see me and talk things over with me, for it is for the hope of Israel that I am wearing this chain." They said to him, " We have received no letter about you from Judaea and none of the brethren has arrived to report or say anything evil about you. We think it right to hear from you what opinions you hold, for, regarding this party of yours, it is a known fact to us that everywhere it is objected to." They fixed a day for him and a considerable number of them came to accept his hospitality. He expounded the matter to them, testifying concerning the Kingdom of God, and trying, from early morning until evening, to persuade them about Jesus with arguments based on the Law of Moses and the Prophets. Some were convinced by what he said and some refused to believe. When they could not agree with one another they began to break up, after Paul had made one last statement, " It was rightly," he said, " that the Holy Spirit spoke to your fathers through the prophet Isaiah saying, ' Go to this people and say, " You will certainly hear and you will surely not understand ; you will certainly look and you will surely not see ; for the heart of this people has grown heavily insensitive and they hear dully with their ears and they have closed their eyes, so that they cannot see with their eyes and hear with their ears and understand with their hearts and turn that I should heal them." Let it be

> known to you, this salvation of God has been sent
> out to the Gentiles ; and it is they who will hear.

THERE is something infinitely wonderful in the fact that
to the end of the day, wherever he went, Paul began with
the Jews. For rather more than thirty years now they
had been doing everything they could to hinder him, to
undo his work, and even to kill him : and even yet it is
to them first he offers his message. Is there any example
of undefeatable hope and unconquerable love like this
act of Paul when, in Rome too, he preached first to the
Jews ? In the end he comes to a conclusion. That conclusion is implied in the quotation from Isaiah which he
uses. His conclusion is that this too is the work of God ;
this very rejection of Jesus by the Jews is the very thing
which has opened the door to the Gentiles. There is a
purpose in everything. On the helm of things there is
the hand of the unseen steersman—God. There is a
double strand all through Acts. On the one side there is
the glory of the way in which the Gentiles accepted Jesus ;
on the other hand there is the tragedy of the way in which
the Jews rejected Him ; but in the strange economy and
in the divine alchemy of God that very tragedy was the
cause of that very triumph. The door which the Jews
shut was the door that opened to the Gentiles ; and even
that is not the end, because some time, at the end of the
day, there will be one flock and one shepherd.

WITHOUT LET OR HINDRANCE

Acts 28 : 30, 31

> For the space of two whole years, Paul remained
> there, earning his own living ; and it was his custom
> to receive all who came to him, preaching the Kingdom
> of God and teaching them the facts about the Lord
> Jesus Christ—with complete freedom of speech and
> without let or hindrance.

To the end of the day Paul is Paul. The Authorised Version
obscures a point. It says that for two years he lived in

his own hired house. The real meaning is that he lived at his own expense ; that he earned his own living. Even in prison his own two hands supplied his need ; he was a burden to no man ; he is independent of all men to the end. And he was not idle. It was there in prison that he wrote the letters to the Philippians, to the Ephesians, to the Colossians and to Philemon. Nor was he ever altogether alone. Luke and Aristarchus had come with him and to the end Luke remained (2 Timothy 4 : 11). Timothy was often with him (Philippians 1 : 1 ; Colossians 1 : 1 ; Philemon 1). Sometimes Tychicus was with him (Ephesians 6 : 21). For a while he had the company of Epaphroditus (Philippians 4 : 18). And sometimes Mark was with him (Colossians 4 : 10). Nor was it wasted time. He tells the Philippians that all this has fallen out to the furtherance of the gospel (Philippians 1 : 12). And specially was that so because, as the translation should be, his bonds were known throughout all the Praetorian Guard (Philippians 1 : 13). He was in his own private lodging but night and day a soldier was with him (Acts 28 : 16). These head-quarters soldiers were members of the picked troops of the Emperor, the Praetorian Guard. In two years many of them must have spent long days and nights with Paul. Paul would never have wasted a chance like that. He and the soldiers must have talked the day and the night away, and many a man must have gone from his guard duty with Christ in his heart. And so the Book of Acts comes to an end with a shout of triumph. In the Greek the words *without let or hindrance* are one word and that one word falls like a victor's cry. It is the peak of Luke's story. We wonder why Luke never told us what happened to Paul, whether he was executed or released. The reason is that that was not Luke's purpose. At the beginning Luke gave us his scheme of Acts when he told us that Jesus commanded His men to preach in Jerusalem and in Judaea and in Samaria and in the uttermost parts of the earth (Acts 1 : 8). The tale is finished ; the story that began in Jerusalem rather more than thirty years ago has finished in Rome. It is nothing less than a miracle of God. The Church which at the beginning of Acts could be numbered in scores cannot now be numbered in tens of thousands. The story of the crucified man of Nazareth has swept across the world in its conquering course until now without let or hindrance it is being preached in Rome, the capital of the world. The gospel has reached the centre of the world and is being freely proclaimed—and Luke's task is at an end.